SCHOLASTIC

SCHOLASTIC Go Grammar

Course Book

Level 6

Page 99: "My Cat is Evil" from *The Undesirable Element* by Justin Plansinis. (http://plantman998.blogspot.com/)
Page 102: "The One that Got Away" from *103 Journeys, Voyages, Trips and Stuff* by Siddhartha Sarma.
Page 105: "The Largest Empire" from *103 Journeys, Voyages, Trips and Stuff* by Siddhartha Sarma.

Published by Scholastic India Pvt. Ltd.
A subsidiary of Scholastic Inc., New York, 10012 (USA)
Publishers since 1920, with international operations in Canada, Australia, New Zealand, the United Kingdom, India, and Hong Kong.

For information regarding permission, write to:
Scholastic India Pvt. Ltd.
A-27, Ground Floor, Bharti Sigma Centre
Infocity-1, Sector 34, Gurgaon (Haryana) 122001
Email: info_in@scholastic.asia

Series editor: Vivek Gopal
Illustrations: Rituparna Sarkar
Layout, design and typesetting: Mansi Bansal

First edition: 2010
Reprinted: 2010, 2011 (four times), 2013 (twice), 2014 (twice), 2015 (twice), 2016 (thrice), 2017 (thrice), 2018, 2019 (four times), 2020, 2021, 2023, 2024

ISBN-13: 978-81-8477-508-2

Contents

Introduction

Being aware of grammar rules enable us to communicate efficiently, clearly and understandably. As human beings, we can put sentences together even as children—we can all *do* grammar. But to be able to talk about how sentences are built, about the types of words and word groups that make up sentences—that is *knowing* about grammar. And *knowing* about grammar offers a window into the human mind and into our amazingly complex culture.

Scholastic Go Grammar 6, 7 and *8* are a series of English grammar course books for the middle-school reader. These books have been created to provide a holistic approach to grammar and language usage that is geared towards practical application over rote memorisation. Simply put, *Scholastic Go Grammar* is a fun approach to grammar that is both instructive and edifying.

The *Scholastic Go Grammar* books

1. Include lesson plans that cover the written and spoken rules of grammar. These include practical solutions for problems that concern even native speakers of English.
2. Have extensive work sheets that engage the student with the rules and exceptions of the English language through practical instances
3. Encourage revision of topics covered in earlier books with more advanced exercises.
4. Include essays, poems, speeches from the finest writers around the world, with an added emphasis on Indian writers. The follow-up comprehension sections dissect how grammar allows these writers to express themselves as well as they do.
5. Incorporate activities that centre around community building in the classroom and events from the student's lives.
6. Provide an exhaustive compilation of supplemental material that is referential and provide a checklist of common writing errors.
7. Follow the current NCERT curriculum and pedagogical principles.
8. Enable educators to monitor students' progress over the course of a lesson through 'free writing' exercises and evaluation sheets provided.

An informative and motivating set of books, *Scholastic Go Grammar* will help students apply the rules of grammar in spoken and written English to make them effective and articulate communicators.

LESSON 1

Nouns

A noun is a word used to name a person, animal, place, thing or an abstract idea. Nouns are often the first words you learn as a child.

➩ teacher, school, book

Kinds of Nouns

Proper Nouns

A proper noun is the special word (or name) that we use for a person, place or organisation. You always write a **proper noun** with a capital letter since the noun represents the name of a specific person, place or thing.

Common Nouns

A **common noun** is a noun referring to a person, place or thing in a general sense. A common noun is the opposite of a proper noun since it lacks specificity. Common nouns are either countable or uncountable.

Common noun	Proper noun
man, boy	John, Suppandi
woman, girl	Aditi, Shruti
country, town	England, London
company	Maruti, Sony
month, day of the week	January, Sunday
book, film	*Malgudi Days, Titanic*

Countable Nouns

Countable nouns are things that we can count. We can count books. We can have one, two, three or more books. Here are some more countable nouns:

➩ dog, cat, animal, person

➩ coin, note, rupee

➩ cup, plate, fork

Nouns

Countable nouns can be singular or plural:

- My dog is playing. (One dog)
- My dogs are hungry. (More than one dog)

When a countable noun is singular, we must use a words **a/the/my/this** with it:

- I want **an** apple. (*not* I want apple.)
- Where is **my** bag? (*not* Where is bag?)

When a countable noun is plural, we can use it by itself:

- I like apples.
- Bags can tear.

We can use **some** and **any** with countable nouns:

- I've got **some** sweets.
- Have you got **any** comics?

We can use a **few** and **many** with countable nouns:

- I've got a **few** pencils.
- I haven't got **many** pens.
- There were very **few** people at the bus stop.

Uncountable Nouns

Uncountable nouns are things that we cannot separate individually. We cannot count them. For example, we cannot count milk. We can count glasses of milk or litres of milk, but we cannot count milk itself. Here are some more uncountable nouns:

- music, art, love, happiness
- advice, information, news
- rice, sugar, butter, water

Nouns

➩ electricity, gas, power

We usually treat uncountable nouns as singular. We use a singular verb.

➩ **This** news **is** very important.

➩ There **is** a lot of water in the Pacific Ocean.

We do not usually use the indefinite article **a/an** with uncountable nouns. We cannot say "an information" or "a happiness". But we can say **a unit of:**

➩ **a piece of** advice

➩ **a glass of** water

➩ **a grain of** rice

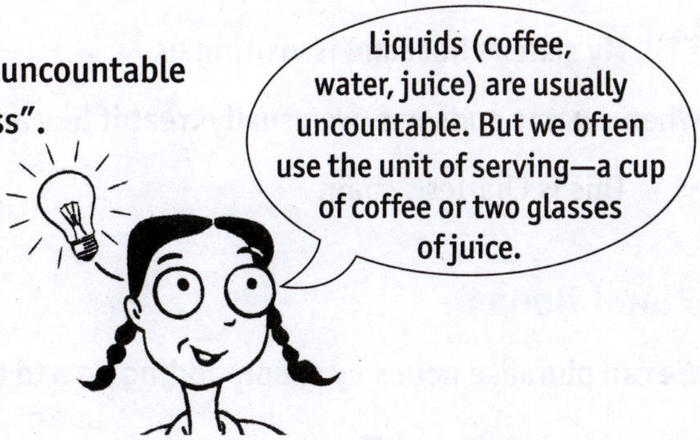

Nouns that can be Countable and Uncountable

Sometimes, the same noun can be countable *and* uncountable, often with a change of meaning.

Countable		Uncountable
There are two lights in our bedroom.	**light**	Close the curtain. There's too much light!
I thought I heard a noise.	**noise**	It's difficult to study when there is too much noise.
Have you got a paper to read?	**paper**	Have you got some paper for me to write on?
Our house has seven rooms.	**room**	Is there room for me to sit here?
We had a great time at the party.	**time**	Have you got time for a coffee?
Macbeth is one of Shakespeare's greatest works.	**work**	I have no money. I need to find work!

Possessives

We add **'s** or **'** to show possession.

Nouns

➩ Vivek's car, my parents' house

Although some writers from earlier times used **of** to show possession, it is now common to use the possessive **'s**. The following sentences mean the same, but the second one is more usual and natural:

➩ The husband of my sister is visiting us.

➩ My sister's husband is visiting us.

When a name ends in **s**, we usually treat it like any other singular noun, and add **'s**:

➩ This is Charles's chair.

Plural Nouns

We can pluralise nouns by simply adding an **s** to them. These are simple plural nouns.

➩ cars, plants, chairs

Irregular Plurals

Some nouns have irregular plural forms without **s**.

➩ wife becomes wives

➩ mosquito becomes mosquitoes

➩ sister-in-law becomes sisters-in-law

➩ mouse becomes mice

To show possession for irregular plural nouns, we simply add **'s** to the plural form of these nouns:

Singular noun	Plural noun
my child's dog	my children's dog
the man's work	the men's work
the mouse's cage	the mice's cage
a person's clothes	people's clothes

Nouns

Noun as Adjective

As you know, a noun is the name of a person, place or thing and an adjective is a word that describes a noun. Sometimes we use a noun to describe another noun. In that case, the first noun acts just like an adjective:

- love story, toothbrush, bathroom

The **noun as adjective** always comes first. If you remember this, it will help you to understand what is being talked about:

- a race horse is a horse that runs in races
- a horse race is a race for horses
- a boat race is a race for boats
- a love story is a story about love
- a war story is a story about war
- a tennis ball is a ball for playing tennis
- tennis shoes are shoes for playing tennis
- a computer exhibition is an exhibition of computers
- a bicycle shop is a shop that sells bicycles

Concrete Nouns

Concrete nouns are things you can touch, feel, smell, taste or hear. These are mostly physical things.

- cat, cheese, songs

Abstract Nouns

Abstract nouns are those that cannot be sensed by our five senses. They usually represent feelings or ideas.

- love, culture, success

WORK SHEET 1

Nouns

Nouns are things. Food (noun) is something you eat. Happiness (noun) is something you feel.

I From the following, pick the correct answer.

1 I ate some (soup made from tomatoes).

a tomato soup *b* soup tomatoes *c* tomatoes soup

2 Tintin has a beautiful (garden of roses).

a roses garden *b* garden roses *c* rose garden

3 My father is growing a (garden of vegetables).

a garden vegetables *b* vegetable garden *c* vegetables garden

4 I got a new (opener for bottles).

a bottles opener *b* opener bottles *c* bottle opener

5 Those were some interesting (articles in a magazine).

a article magazine *b* magazine articles *c* magazines article

6 Shawna plays (games on the computer) every Saturday.

a computers games *b* games computer *c* computer games

7 Cats shouldn't sit on the (tables in the kitchen).

a kitchen tables *b* table kitchen *c* kitchens table

8 Where is the (device that controls the TV remotely)?

a control remote *b* remote control *c* device remote

9 The children like (ice cream made from strawberries).

a ice cream strawberry *b* strawberry ice cream *c* strawberries ice cream

10 I watched a good (programme on television) after work.

a television programme *b* programme television *c* televisions programmes

Nouns

Concrete nouns are the names of things you can touch, taste, feel, hear or smell. They name real and solid things. For example: chocolate, bicycle, rain

I Pick the correct word.

1 My father said that ____________ going to snow later today.

a it's *b* it *c* its

2 I always carry ____________ of my dog.

a pictures' *b* picture's *c* pictures

3 Charlie, Rajesh and Sachin were playing. Lucie came and kicked the ________ ball away.

a boys' *b* boys *c* boy's

4 I have seen ____________ before.

a it's *b* it *c* its

5 Where did you say you left ____________ bike?

a you're *b* you *c* your

6 I ____________ see anything from the back of the theatre.

a couldnt *b* could'nt *c* couldn't

7 ____________ leaving in five minutes.

a We're *b* Wer'e *c* Were

8 A snake uses ____________ tongue to sense motion around it.

a it's *b* it *c* its

9 The ____________ nice today.

a weather *b* weather's *c* weathers'

10 ____________ name is Dr Livingstone, isn't it?

a Your *b* You're *c* Yours

11 ____________ my best friend.

a You *b* You're *c* Your

12 We only sell ____________ in this shop.

a apples' *b* apple's *c* apples

LESSON 2

Pronouns

Pronouns are words that can be used in place of a noun.
Without pronouns, we would repeat a lot of nouns.

With pronouns, we can say:

➩ Do you like Lakshmi? I don't like **her. She** is too pompous.

Pronouns can be of several types:

Life without pronouns

Personal Pronouns

Personal pronouns represent specific people or things. We use personal pronouns in place of the person or people that we are talking about.

➩ **I** like coffee.

➩ Do **you** like coffee?

➩ Did Ram beat **him**?

Demonstrative Pronouns

A demonstrative pronoun represents things that are:

- near in distance or time (**this, these**)
- far in distance or time (**that, those**)

	Near	Far
singular	this	that
plural	these	those

Pronouns

Here are some examples with demonstrative pronouns:

- **Have you seen this?** → Have you seen **this**?
- **These** are bad times.
- **That** is beautiful.
- **Those** were the days!

That and **which** are often used interchangeably where **that** often implies proximity (with regard to time or space) between the speaker and the object. The relation between the speaker and the object is made less prominent through the use of **which**.

- This is the house that has a broken window.
- This is the house, which has a broken window.

In the former sentence, **that** implies that the primary trait of the house is the broken window. In the second sentence, the house is pointed out as having a broken window, but not defined by it.

Interrogative Pronouns

We use interrogative pronouns to ask questions. Interrogative pronouns are used to find out information about things that we don't know (what we are asking the question about):

- **Whoever** would want to do such a thing?
- **Whatever** did he say to make her laugh like that?

Possessive Pronouns

We use possessive pronouns to imply ownership or belonging to a specific person/people or thing/things:

- Jordan found his books but Mary couldn't find **hers**. (object = her books)
- Here is your bat. **Ours** is over there, where we left it. (subject = Our bat)
- I don't like this family's garden but I like **yours**. (object = garden)

LESSON 2

Pronouns

Reflexive Pronouns

We use a reflexive pronoun when we want to refer back to the subject of the sentence or clause:

- I saw **myself** in the mirror.
- Why do you blame **yourself**?
- Can you help **yourselves**?

Note: the underlined words refer to the same person/thing.

Reciprocal Pronouns

Reciprocal pronouns refer to individual parts of a preceding plural noun.

There are only two reciprocal pronouns:

- Each other (used when there are two people involved)
- One another (used when there are three or more people involved)

Remember that reciprocal pronouns are used for cases where there are:

- **two or more** people, things or groups involved (so we cannot use I, you [singular], he/she/it), and
- they must be **doing the same thing**

Look at these examples:

- Peter and David hate **each other.**
- The children were all blaming **one another.**
- Both teams played hard against **each other.**
- We gave **each other** gifts.
- The prisoners were fighting **one another.**

Indefinite Pronouns

An indefinite pronoun does not refer to any specific person, thing or amount. It can encompass a wide range of people, events or places.

Pronouns

Example of indefinite pronouns are: all, another, any, anybody/anyone, anything, each, everybody/ everyone, everything, few, many, nobody, none, one, several, some, somebody/someone

Most indefinite pronouns are either singular or plural. However, some of them can be singular in one context and plural in another:

➩ **Each** of the players *has* a doctor.

➩ **Two** schools of fish *were* swimming. **Each** went *their* own way.

➩ I met two girls. **One** *has* given me *her* phone number.

Similarly, plural pronouns need plural verbs and that any personal pronoun should also agree with the plural case.

➩ **Many** *have* expressed *their* views.

Singular pronoun	Meaning	Examples
another	an additional or different person or thing	That ice cream was good. Can I have **another**?
anybody/anyone	no matter what person	Can **anyone** answer this question?
either	one or the other of two people or things	Do you want tea or coffee? / I don't mind. **Either** is good for me.
everything	all things	They have no house or possessions. They lost **everything** in the earthquake.
less	a smaller amount	We received **less** rainfall than the previous year.
little	a small amount	**Little** is known about his early life.
much	a large amount	**Much** has happened since last year.
one	an unidentified person	All the students arrived but now **one** is missing.
other	a different person or thing from one already mentioned	One was tall and the **other** was short.

LESSON 2

Pronouns

Singular pronoun	Meaning	Examples
somebody/someone	an unspecified or unknown person	Clearly **somebody** murdered him.
something	an unspecified or unknown thing	Listen! I just heard **something**! What could it be?
you	an unidentified person (informal)	And **you** can see why.

Plural pronoun	Meaning	Examples
both	two people or things, seen together	Vivek likes coffee but not tea. I think **both** are good.
fewer	a reduced number of people or things	**Fewer** people are reading these days.
others	other people; not us	I'm sure that **others** have tried before us.
several	more than two but not many	They all complained and **several** left the meeting.

Singular or plural pronoun	Meaning	Examples
all	the whole quantity of something or of some things or people	**All** is forgiven. **All** have arrived.
most	the majority; nearly all	**Most** is lost. **Most** have refused.
none	not any; no person or persons	They fixed the water, so why is **none** coming out of the tap? I invited five friends but **none** have come.

WORK SHEET 3

Pronouns

A pronoun can replace a noun or another pronoun.
For example: Mansi takes **her** dog for a walk. **She** takes **it** to the park.

I Tick the sentences that are correct. Rewrite the sentences that have errors.

1 Ameet, Vishal and myself are headed home now. ☐

____

2 Give the books to myself. ☐

____

3 She wrote that essay all by herself. ☐

____

4 They were concerned for theirselves in such a dangerous situation. ☐

____

5 He just has to learn that for hisself. ☐

____

6 I want him to do the job himself. ☐

____

7 I myself believe that also. ☐

____

8 The players themselves are willing to play for free. ☐

____

9 She asked herself some difficult questions. ☐

____

10 He gave hisself a treat for being good. ☐

____

Pronouns

Remember, unlike nouns, personal pronouns have different forms for masculine, feminine and neuter genders.

I Choose between the reflexive pronoun, the reciprocal pronoun (each other) or nothing.

1 Kartik hurt when climbing the tree.

____

2 Peter and I helped finish our homework.

____

3 I enjoyed at the swings today.

____

4 Did she make a tasty milkshake?

____

5 The wild monkey looked at in the mirror.

____

6 Thompson and Thomson smiled at.

____

7 We're meeting at the railway station.

____

8 During class, Jane and Mary were talking to.

____

9 I don't remember where we spent our holiday last year.

____

10 We need to cooperate with.

____

Pronouns

Indefinite pronouns refer to an identifiable but not specified person or thing.

I Circle the indefinite pronoun.

1 Everything was calm before the storm.

2 Many came to see what had happened.

3 None knew what to do.

4 Somebody knocked at the door.

5 Few responded to my party invitation.

II Circle the correct possessive pronoun.

1 This is a nice pen. Is it your / yours ?

2 That is not mine / my book. My / Mine has my name on it.

3 Whose umbrella is this? Your / Yours or my / mine ?

4 Tina is going our with her / hers friends this evening.

5 My / Mine car is bigger than her / hers.

6 They have two kittens but I don't know their / theirs names.

7 Can we use your car? Our / Ours is broken.

8 Pooja's room is red. Mine / My is blue.

9 The dog wags it / its tail.

10 The pictures are her / hers.

Pronouns

Possessive pronouns show who owns a particular object.

I Complete the following sentences with the correct possessive pronoun.

1 Priya left ______________ bag on the bus.

a her *b* yours *c* his

2 The drawings on the wall are by ______________ son.

a their *b* your *c* mine

3 The winners brought home ______________ prizes.

a his *b* her *c* their

4 The warm bread just melts in ______________ mouth.

a your *b* mine *c* its

5 That puppy is not ______________.

a mine *b* their *c* her

6 I had never tried that flavour before; so Tina let me taste ______________.

a mine *b* hers *c* its

7 No, that book is ______________.

a mine *b* yours *c* theirs

8 Children, where are ______________ English books?

a your *b* mine *c* their

9 Arti and I like pizza. It is ______________ favourite food.

a her *b* our *c* mine

10 The boys are playing with ______________ football.

a his *b* your *c* their

WORK SHEET 7

Pronouns

The demonstrative pronouns **this** and **these** refer to things that are nearby in space or in time; **that** and **those** refer to things further away in space or time.

I Complete the following sentences with the appropriate demonstrative pronoun. There may be more than one correct answer.

1 ______________ pair of shoes is not mine.

2 ______________ stuffed monkeys over there look real.

3 ______________ jeans fit me well.

4 There are a lot of problems with ______________ article.

5 ______________ flowers look beautiful.

6 The characters in ______________ movie were not likeable.

7 Shall I take ______________ books from your desk?

8 Were you serious about letting me borrow ______________ books?

9 ______________ classrooms are full of tiny chairs.

10 ______________ paintings in the restaurant were terrible.

11 ______________ soup tasted like soap.

12 ______________ belong to Ramona.

13 ______________ tastes delicious.

Articles

The good news is that there are only three articles in English: **a**, **an** and **the**.

Indefinite Articles

A and **an** are indefinite articles. They are used before nouns that introduce something or someone who has not been mentioned before:

- I saw **an** elephant the other day.
- I am **a** student at this school.

We use **a** when the noun we are referring to begins with a consonant (b, c, d, f, g, h, j, k, l, m, n, p, q, r, s, t, v, w, x, y or z).

- **a** city, **a** factory and **a** hotel

We use **an** when the noun we are referring to begins with a vowel (a, e, i, o, u)

- **an** egg, **an** ultimatum

Pronunciation changes this rule.

- **a** university
- **an** honourable peace
- **a** union
- **an** honest mistake

In such cases, it is the letter being stressed in pronunciation that determines the article.

Definite Article

We use **the** when we know that the listener knows or can work out what particular person or thing we are talking about.

- Could you pass me **the** book on **the** table?

We should also use **the** when we have already mentioned the thing we are talking about.

Articles

➩ She's got two children; **a** girl and **a** boy. **The** girl's six and **the** boy's eight.

We use **the** to talk about geographical points on the globe.

➩ **the** North Pole

We use **the** to talk about rivers, oceans and seas

➩ **the** Ganga, **the** Atlantic Ocean

We also use **the** before certain nouns when we know there is only one of a particular thing.

➩ **the** Taj Mahal, **the** sun

We do not use an article before the names of countries ***except*** where they indicate multiple areas or contain the words [state(s), kingdom, republic, union]. Kingdom, state, republic and union are nouns, so they need an article:

➩ **the** United States of America, **the** United Kingdom

The is also a **determiner**. It is placed before a noun to indicate whether you are referring to something specific or something of a particular type.

the definite article	the
demonstratives	this, that, these, those
possessives	my, your, his, her, its, our, their

WORK SHEET 8

Articles

We use **a** or **an** when we don't specify which things or people we are talking about.

I Complete the sentences with a suitable article.

1 Albert Einstein was ______________ famous scientist.

2 Einstein won ______________ Nobel Prize in Physics in 1921.

3 Mother Teresa was ______________ Roman Catholic nun.

4 Mother Teresa became famous for her hard work with ______________ poor.

5 Mother Teresa lived in ______________ city of Kolkata.

6 Don't stay in that hotel. ______________ beds are very uncomfortable.

7 My father is returning from ______________ Republic of Ireland.

8 That is ______________ university where I study.

9 My mother is ______________ English teacher.

10 Her house is ______________ hour's drive from here.

II Complete the following sentences with a suitable word.

1 I went to the museum and saw a ______________.

2 We bought tickets to see the ______________.

3 He is an ______________ gentleman.

4 Shilpa has a ______________ dog.

5 My brother was driving at 100 kilometres an ______________.

6 She has an ______________ in Hyderabad.

7 Can I have an ______________?

8 Shantanu is one of the ______________ people I know.

Adjectives

An adjective is a word that tells us more about a noun.

There are two basic positions for adjectives:

- **before** the noun
- **after** certain **verbs** (be, become, get, seem, look, feel, sound, smell, taste)

	Adjective	Noun	Verb	Adjective
I like	big	cars.		
		My car	is	big.

Comparative Adjectives

We can use comparative adjectives when we want to compare a noun to something else (smarter, taller). There are two ways to make or form a comparative adjective:

- **short** adjectives: add **er** to the end of the word
- **long** adjectives: use **more**

⇨ America is big. But Russia is **bigger**.

⇨ I want to have a **more** powerful computer.

Exceptions

The following adjectives have irregular forms:

- good → better
- well (healthy) → better
- bad → worse
- far → farther/further

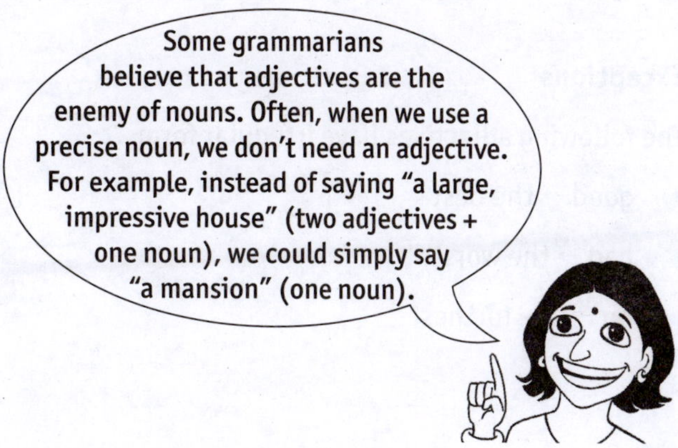

Adjectives

Superlative Adjectives

Superlative adjectives are the highest degree of a particular group. They tend to precede any other adjectives.

➩ My English teacher is the **nicest** teacher in school.

➩ This painting is the **worst**.

We can form a superlative by:

Form	Rule	Examples
Single syllable words ending in **e**.	Add **st** to the end of the word.	nice → nicest
Single syllable words ending in a consonant.	Double the consonant and add **est** to the end of the word.	big → biggest
Single syllable words with more than one vowel or more than one consonant in the end.	Add **est** to the end of the word.	high → highest
Two syllable words ending in **y**.	Change **y** to **i** and add **est** to the end of the word.	happy → happiest
Two or more syllable words not ending in **y**.	Place **the most** before the adjective.	beautiful → the most beautiful

Exceptions

The following adjectives have irregular forms.

- good → the best
- bad → the worst
- far → the furthest

Adjectives

Adjectives modify a noun or pronoun by describing or quantifying them.

I Complete the following sentences with the appropriate words.

1 Chandra never helps around the house. He's so ____________!

2 Aishwarya was ____________ of Linda. She was much better at sports than Aishwarya.

3 Janice rarely gets angry with people. She's very ____________ and understanding.

4 My dog is very ____________. I'm sure you'll like her when you meet her.

5 The teacher felt very ____________ when all her students did well in the exam.

6 My friend Raina is very ____________. She is good at learning different things.

7 People who push in front of you in queues are very ____________!

8 My sister Pooja is ____________. I'm the opposite. I'm not very bright.

9 My brother Ekrem is very ____________. His desk is always tidy.

10 Our neighbour is a good person. She has been very ____________ to us.

11 I hate working in the coal mine. It is so ____________ down there.

12 The apple I bit into was very ____________.

13 The acrobat Philippe Petit is famous for his tightrope act. He must be incredibly ____________ to do such a thing.

14 This horse is far too ____________.

15 There are many ____________ sausages in Germany.

WORK SHEET 10

Adjectives

Adjectives often precede the noun or pronoun they are modifying.

I Fill in the correct comparative or superlative forms of the words in brackets.

1 My room is (big) ____________________ than yours.

2 This painting is (beautiful) ____________________ than that one.

3 This is the (interesting) ____________________ book I have ever read.

4 Cats usually live (long) ____________________ than dogs.

5 Which is the (poisonous) ____________________ snake in the world?

6 A holiday by the beach is (good) ____________________ than a holiday in the mountains.

7 It is strange but a motorcycle can be (expensive) ____________________ than a car.

8 Who is the (rich) ____________________ woman in India?

9 The heat this summer is even (bad) ____________________ than last summer.

10 He was the (clever) ____________________ thief of all.

11 The yellow hat is (bright) ____________________ than the sun.

12 Ramdas is the (bore) ____________________ person I've ever met.

13 The Alps are very high. They are the (high) ____________________ mountains in Europe.

14 A Rolls Royce is (expensive) ____________________ than an Atlas cycle.

15 This question is not difficult. It's (easy) ____________________ than you think.

Adverbs

As you remember, adverbs are words that give meaning to verbs, adjectives or other adverbs.

We can usually recognise an adverb by its function (job), manner or position.

Function

The primary job or function of an adverb is to modify (give us more information about) verbs, adjectives and other adverbs.

- Modify a verb:

➡ She *speaks* **loudly**. (How does she speak?)

➡ He *lives* **locally**. (Where does he live?)

➡ She **never** *studies*. (When does she study?)

- Modify an adjective:

➡ He is **really** *handsome*.

- Modify another adverb:

➡ She drives **incredibly** *slowly*.

Adverbs can also:

- Modify a whole sentence:

➡ **Obviously**, *I can't know everything*.

- Modify a prepositional phrase:

➡ It's **immediately** *inside the door*.

Manner

Many adverbs end in **ly**. We form such adverbs by adding **ly** to the adjective.

➡ The kitten landed **softly** on the stairs.

But not all words that end in **ly** are adverbs. **Friendly**, for example, is an adjective.

LESSON 5

Adverbs

Some adverbs have no particular form.

➩ He is **often** late for class.

Position

Adverbs have three main positions in a sentence:

- Front (before the subject):

➩ **Now** we will study adverbs.

- Middle (between the subject and the main verb):

➩ We **often** study adverbs.

- End (after the verb or object):

➩ We study adverbs **carefully**.

Kinds of Adverbs

Adverbs of Time

These tell us when things happen:

➩ Do it **now**.

➩ I will see you **then**.

➩ She told me **yesterday**.

Adverbs of Frequency

These adverbs tell us how frequently or how often some actions occur:

100%	always
	usually
75%	frequently
	often
50%	sometimes
	occasionally
	rarely
25%	seldom
	hardly ever
0%	never

➩ He **never** completes his homework.

➩ She **always** writes neatly.

➩ We **sometimes** play in the park.

Adverbs

Interrogative Adverbs

These are:

who, why, where, how, when

They are usually placed at the ***beginning of a question***.

- **Why** are you so late?
- **Where** is my Maths book?
- **How** are you?

Adverbs of Degree

Adverbs of degree tell us about the intensity of an action.

- The water was **extremely** cold.
- She has **just** finished reading.

Adverbs

Adverbs are words that describe verbs.

I Rewrite the complete sentence using the adverb in brackets in its proper position.

1 Our class must write an essay. (**also**)

____

2 I was joking about putting a lizard in her shoe. (**only**)

____

3 Did you enjoy the trip? (**both**)

____

4 My grandmother watches TV. (**hardly**) (**ever**)

____

5 He composes his e-mail. (**carefully**)

____

6 The children play cricket. (**in the garden**)

____

7 We went to the theatre. (**yesterday**)

____

8 Aditya fell off the bike yesterday. (**almost**)

____

9 Her uncle will buy her some sweets. (**probably**)

____

10 My cousin is moving to Singapore soon. (**definitely**)

____

WORK SHEET 12

Adverbs

Adverbs often convey a greater or lesser emphasis to something. For example: I **really** don't trust him.

I Read each sentence. Decide whether the underlined adverb is describing when, where or how an action happens. Write how, when or where on each line.

1 Karsh quickly ate his lunch. ____________

2 Aparna often watches movies about vampires. ____________

3 Olivia immediately came to the garden. ____________

4 When will you come here to visit us? ____________

5 Gopal slowly walked to the sweet shop. ____________

6 Sometimes Jessica goes to the museum. ____________

7 Please speak clearly and loudly. ____________

8 Hugo went inside the abandoned house. ____________

9 Vandana neatly wrote a shopping list. ____________

10 I carefully glued the last piece onto the boat. ____________

WORK SHEET 13

Adverbs

We often use **more** and **most**, **less** and **least** to show degree with adverbs. For example: This is the **most** boring task I have ever done.

I Complete the sentences with the correct adjective or adverb. Tick the box to indicate which it is.

1 The guard shouted ______________ at him. ☐ adjective ☐ adverb

a angry *b* angrily

2 He is a ______________ student. ☐ adjective ☐ adverb

a careless *b* carelessly

3 If you ask ______________, I will buy you ice cream. ☐ adjective ☐ adverb

a nice *b* nicely

4 Be quiet! I can't think ______________ if you are shouting. ☐ adjective ☐ adverb

a clear *b* clearly

5 Why are you ______________? ☐ adjective ☐ adverb

a grumpy *b* grumpily

6 You are being really ______________ today. ☐ adjective ☐ adverb

a slow *b* slowly

7 These chocolates look ______________. Can I have one? ☐ adjective ☐ adverb

a delicious *b* deliciously

8 She opened the door ______________. ☐ adjective ☐ adverb

a slow *b* slowly

9 It is a beautiful ______________ day. ☐ adjective ☐ adverb

a clear *b* clearly

10 You write so ______________. Look at these mistakes. ☐ adjective ☐ adverb

a careless *b* carelessly

Adverbs

Adverbs can often be identified by their characteristic **ly** suffix.

I Based on the percentage provided, rewrite the following with adverbs of frequency.

1 Anita and I (30%) go out for coffee together.

____

2 Neha (90%) has ice cream for dessert.

____

3 I (20%) drive my car to work.

____

4 My sister eats vegetables (100%).

____

5 It (0%) rains here in the summer.

____

6 We take the dog off his leash (70%) at the beach.

____

7 My sister takes a day off school (5%).

____

8 My parents and I take vacations together (80%) quite .

____

9 Varun (10%) gets to visit his cousins.

____

10 I (0%) went to college.

____

Conjunctions

Conjunctions join words and ideas together in a cohesive way.

- I came early **so that** I could talk to you privately.

The two concepts being joined are the person coming in early and wanting to talk privately.

Conjunctions have three basic forms:

Single Word

These are single word conjunctions that connect two or more words.

- I want to go to the kitchen **and** get milk.

Compound Word

These are several words or phrases that join ideas.

- I'll come **as long as** you drive.

Correlative

These conjunctions show how two parts of the sentence correlate to each other.

- I am so kind **that** I will drive you.

Coordinating conjunctions are used to join parts of a sentence that are grammatically equal.

The two parts of the sentence that are joined together may be single words or clauses:

- Jack **and** Jill went up the hill.
- The water was warm, **but** I didn't go swimming.

Subordinating conjunctions are words that connect two thoughts by making one subordinate to the other, or by making one statement less important than the other.

- I went swimming **although** it was cold.
- I'll look after the animals **while** you're away.

LESSON 6

Conjunctions

The following is a list of the most common subordinating conjunctions.

after	even though	that
although	how	though
as	if	till (or 'til)
as if	in as much	unless
as long as	in order that	until
as much as	lest	when
as soon as	now that	whenever
as though	provided (that)	where
because	since	wherever
before	so that	while
even if	than	

Conjunctions

Conjunctions are parts of speech that connect words, phrases or clauses together.

I Underline the conjunctions in the following sentences.

1 Since I couldn't go swimming, I watched a movie.

2 We had lots of fun until the teacher came.

3 We ate lots of sweets that made us sick.

4 I ate ice cream while my mother was shopping.

5 It will rain as it looks very cloudy today.

6 Unless you finish your work, you can't play.

7 Although he knew it was difficult, he tried anyway.

8 She would have cried if she were hurt.

9 He is crying because he is sad.

10 I like her because she has always been nice to me.

11 He warned me not to eat that, but I did not listen.

12 You cannot be a pirate until you get a parrot.

13 You can either take it or leave it.

14 I would like to dance but I am too clumsy.

15 Would you like coffee or tea?

Conjunctions

The conjunction **and** is used when the words or phrases being joined are of equal importance.

I Choose the correct answer for each sentence.

1 You can come with me ______________ you don't say anything.

a so that *b* as long as *c* while *d* until

2 I'm not leaving ______________ I get my kite back.

a so that *b* as long as *c* while *d* until

3 I came here ______________ you could have an alibi.

a so that *b* as long as *c* while *d* until

4 Ameet is very tall ______________ Mahima is very short.

a so that *b* as long as *c* while *d* as if

5 You look ______________ you've seen a ghost.

a as long as *b* while *c* as long as *d* as if

6 You look ______________ you haven't eaten for a week.

a so that *b* as if *c* while *d* until

7 I don't mind if you go out to play ______________ you're back for lunch at two.

a so that *b* as long as *c* while *d* until

8 ______________ being a mime is very interesting, it's also very badly paid.

a So that *b* As long as *c* While *d* Until

9 We'll go to Shimla on Saturday ______________ it doesn't rain.

a so that *b* as long as *c* while *d* as if

10 ______________ I don't approve of what you did, I know you meant well.

a So that *b* As long as *c* While *d* Until

Prepositions

A **preposition** is a word that is usually placed before a noun or pronoun to express its relation to another word or element:

- She left **before** breakfast.
- What did you come **for**?

There is one very simple rule about prepositions. This rule has no exceptions.

A preposition is followed by a noun. It is never followed by a verb.

- She lives **in** Japan.
- Tara is looking **for** you.

According to the rule, the following sentence should not be possible:

- I would like to go now.

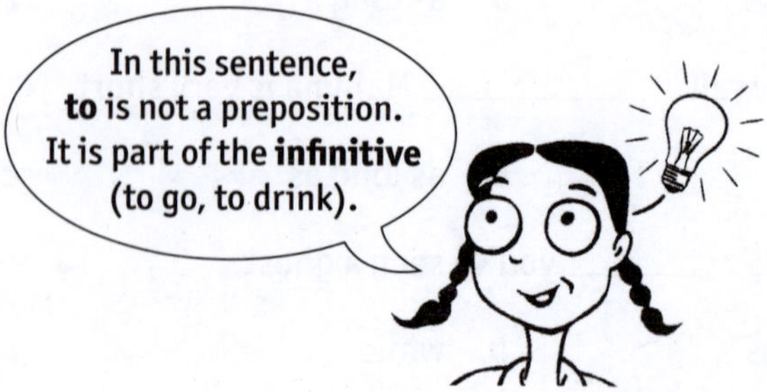

Prepositions of Time

We use:

- **at** for a precise time
- **in** for months, years, centuries and long periods
- **on** for days and dates

- I have a meeting **at** 9 am.
- Do you work **on** Mondays?
- Sonia went home **at** lunchtime.
- In Kashmir, it often snows **in** December.

LESSON 7

Prepositions

Prepositions of Place

In general, we use:

- **at** for a point
- **in** for an enclosed space
- **on** for a surface

➩ Revathi is waiting for you **at** the bus stop.

➩ The shop is **at** the end of the street.

➩ My plane stopped **at** Dubai and Hanoi and arrived **in** Bangkok two hours late.

➩ Be **on** time for your bus.

Location	Time	Action and movement
above	at	at
below	on	by
over	by	from
under	before	into
among	from	on
between	since	onto
beside	for	off
in front of	during	out of
behind	to	
next to	until	
with	after	
in the middle of		
on		
in		
at		

WORK SHEET 17

Prepositions

Prepositions show relationship between nouns in a sentence through direction, place, cause, time and amount.

I Complete the sentences with the correct prepositions.

1 He made his escape by jumping ______ a window and jumping ______ a waiting car.

2 I saw something about it ______ television.

3 I couldn't get in ______ the door so I had to climb ______ a window.

4 He drove ______ me without stopping and drove off ______ the centre of town.

5 I went ______ him and asked him the best way to get ______ Jaipur.

6 He was driving ______ 180 miles per hour when he crashed ______ the central barrier.

7 She ran ______ the corridor and ______ the stairs to the second floor.

8 When the bull ran ______ me, I jumped ______ the fence.

9 Look, that car's ______ fire.

10 He took the book ______ the shelf and put it ______ his bag.

11 I live ______ Norway.

12 Who is this person ______ this picture?

13 Many tourists shop ______ Janpath.

14 She will call you ______ 2:30 pm.

15 Her silly hat was ______ my face.

Prepositions

Prepositions indicate the relationship of its object to the rest of the sentence.

I The prepositions in the sentences below are incorrect. Rewrite the sentences with the correct preposition.

1 We saw the plane flying under the bridge.

____

2 Don't play football after the house.

____

3 The dog dug a hole between the ground.

____

4 Were you asleep under the alarm clock rang?

____

5 The ball rolled up the hill.

____

6 The seagull glided beneath the water.

____

7 He was proud of his marks on the examination.

____

8 According with Neeraj, there's something wrong.

____

9 I'll introduce you on them for a minute or two.

____

10 For whom do these English books belong?

____

LESSON 8

Verb Tense

Tenses are tools that allow us to show the passage of time.

There are three basic tenses. These are present tense, past tense and future tense.

Simple Present Tense

We use the simple present tense when:

- the action is general

LESSON 8

Verb Tense

- the action happens all the time, or habitually, in the past, present and future
- the statement is always true

➲ I like coffee.

➲ The moon goes round the earth.

➲ Rohini is Vijay's sister.

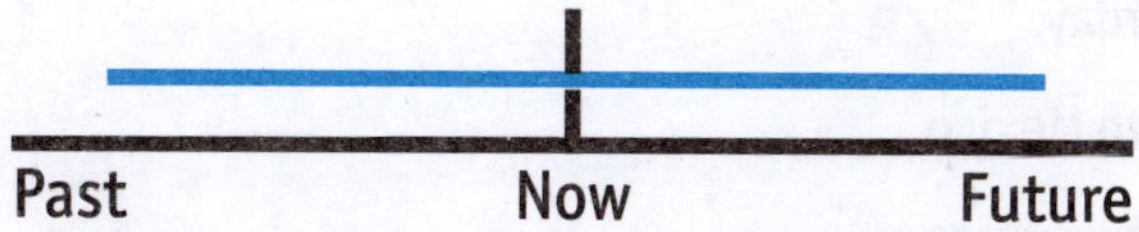

The simple present tense can also be used to talk about scheduled events in the near future.

➲ The train **leaves** tonight at 6 pm.

➲ When **do** we **board** the plane?

Present Continuous Tense

The present continuous tense is used to express the idea that something is happening (or not happening) now, at this very moment.

➲ You **are watching** TV.

➲ You **are not swimming** now.

Sometimes, speakers use the present continuous to indicate that something will or will not happen in the near future.

➲ I **am meeting** some friends after lunch.

➲ **Isn't** she **coming** with us tonight?

LESSON 8

Verb Tense

Simple Past Tense

You've already learnt that we use the past tense of a verb to show an action that has already occurred.

We use simple past tense to show that an action started and finished at a specific time in the past.

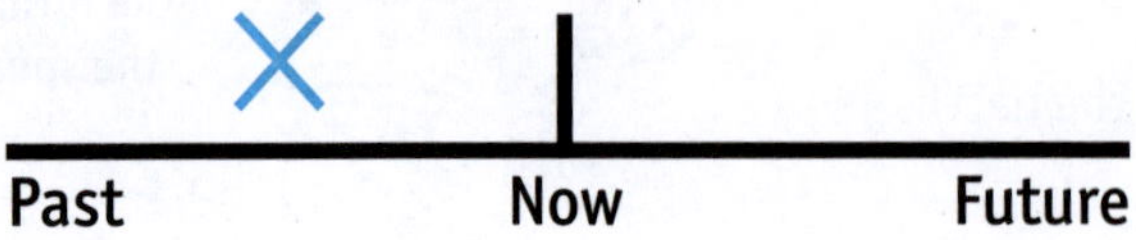

- I **ate** lunch.
- We **saw** a movie yesterday.
- Last year, I **travelled** to Mexico.
- I **lived** in Mumbai for two years.

Past Perfect Tense

The past perfect tense is used to show an action that got completed before some specified time in the past.

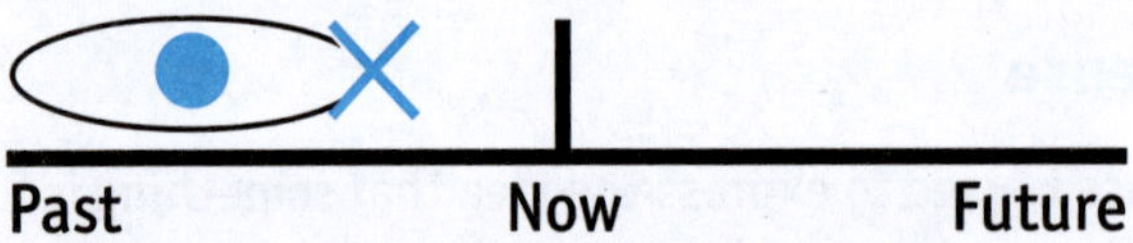

- The wind **blew** away the leaves that we **had collected**.

Blew is simple past as it is an action in the past. **Had collected** indicates that this action (collecting leaves) took place before the wind blew them away.

- You had **studied** English before you **moved** to New Delhi.

Past Continuous Tense

We use the past continuous tense to show a past action over a period of time.

- I **was watching** television.

Verb Tense

We use the past continuous tense with words such as **always** to talk about things that happened repeatedly.

➩ She **was always coming** to class late.

The past continuous is also used to show two actions occurring at the same time.

➩ I **was watching** TV while he **was making** dinner.

We can use the past continuous tense and the simple past tense together to show an action that was interrupted.

➩ He **called** when I **was watching** TV.

Sentences can be active or passive. Therefore, tenses also have **active forms** and **passive forms.** These forms can be used to emphasise different parts of the sentence.

Future Tense

As you remember, we use **simple future** to show an action that will occur at some point in time.

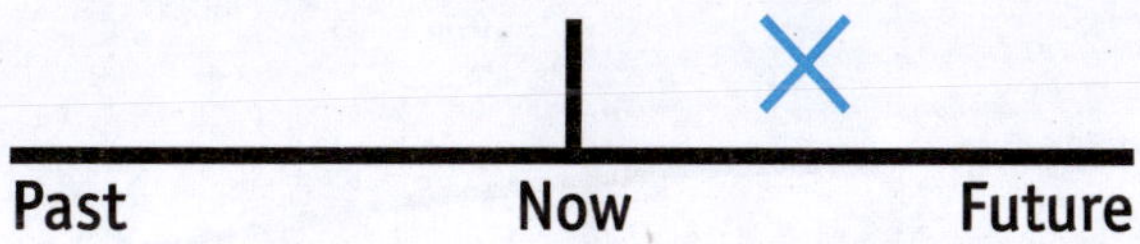

➩ She **is going** to the dentist on Tuesday.

➩ It **will rain** tomorrow.

Future Perfect Tense

The future perfect tense indicates that something will occur before another action in the future.

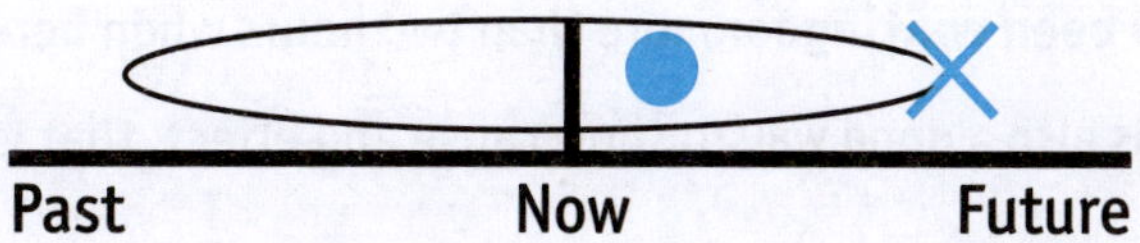

➩ By next week I **will have finished** my exams.

Verb Tense

The future perfect tense is composed of two parts: the simple future of the verb to have (will have) + the past participle of the main verb **finished.**

The future perfect has two different forms: **will have done** and **be going to have done.**

Will have + [past participle] is used when something will occur before another action in the future or when something will happen before a specific time in the future.

- By next November, I will have received my promotion.
- By the time I finish this course, I will have taken four exams.

Going to have + [past participle} is commonly used when an action started in the past will only finish or occur in the future.

- By Monday, she is going to have had my book for a week.
- I am going to have been in this school for five years next month.

Future Perfect Continuous Tense

We use the future perfect continuous tense to show an action or an event long before some point in the future.

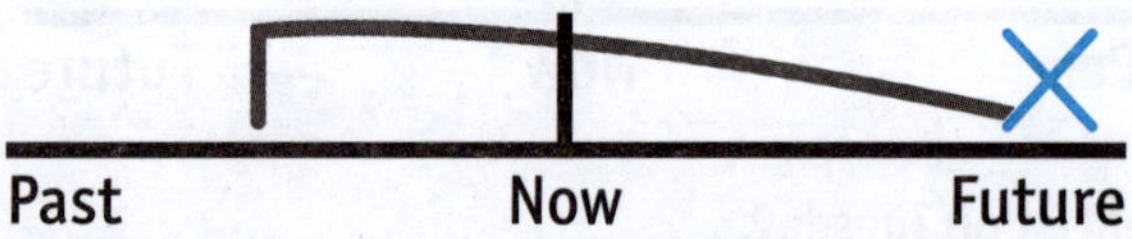

- I **will have been studying** here for ten years next year.

The future perfect continuous tense has two different forms: **will have been doing** and **be going to have been doing.**

- You **will have been waiting** for more than two hours when her plane arrives.
- You are **going to have been waiting** for more than two hours when her plane arrives.

Future perfect continuous is also a good way to show cause and effect, that is, why something happened.

- Ram will be tired when he gets home because he **will have been jogging** for over an hour.

Verb Tense

For negative sentences in the future perfect continuous tense, we insert **not** between **will** and **have.** For question sentences, we exchange the subject and **will.**

- We will **not** have been waiting long.
- Will you have been watching TV?

Active Voice

In active sentences, the person or thing doing the action is the subject of the sentence and the thing receiving the action is the object.

- Lakshmi **gave** back the book.

[thing/person doing action] + [verb] + [thing/person receiving action]

Passive Voice

In passive sentences, the person or thing receiving the action is the subject of the sentence and the thing doing the action is optionally included near the end of the sentence.

- The book **was given** back by Lakshmi.

[thing/person receiving action] + [be] + [past participle of verb] + [by] + [thing/person doing action]

Verb Tense

Active/Passive Overview

Tense	Active	Passive
Simple present	Once a week, Neeraj **cleans** the room.	Once a week, the room **is cleaned** by Neeraj.
Present continuous	Right now, Pooja **is writing** the letter.	Right now, the letter **is being written** by Pooja.
Simple past	Vikas **repaired** the car.	The car **was repaired** by Vikas.
Past continuous	The salesman **was helping** the customer when the boss came into the store.	The customer **was being helped** by the salesman when the boss came into the store.
Present perfect	Many tourists **have visited** that temple.	That temple **has been visited** by many tourists.
Present perfect continuous	Mohan **has been doing** the work.	The work **has been done** by Mohan.
Past perfect	Vinay **had repaired** many computers before he received his engineering degree.	Many computers **had been repaired** by Vinay before he received his engineering degree.
Past perfect continuous	I **had been cooking** dinner.	Dinner **had been cooked** by me.
Simple future *will*	Someone **will finish** the work by 5:00 pm.	The work **will be finished** by someone by 5:00 pm.
Simple future *be going to*	Parul **is going to make** a sumptuous dinner tonight.	A sumptuous dinner **is going to be made by** Parul tonight.
Future continuous *will*	At 8:00 pm tonight, Varun **will be washing** the dishes.	At 8:00 pm tonight, the dishes **will be washed** by Varun.

LESSON 8

Verb Tense

Tense	Active	Passive
Future continuous *be going to*	At 8:00 pm tonight, Varun **is going to be washing** the dishes.	At 8:00 pm tonight, the dishes **are going to be washed** by Varun.
Future perfect *will*	They **will have completed** the project before the deadline.	The project **will have been completed** before the deadline.
Future perfect *be going to*	They **are going to have completed** the project before the deadline.	The project **is going to have been completed** before the deadline.
Future perfect continuous *will*	The artist **will have been painting** the mural for over six months by the time it is finished.	The mural **will have been being painted** by the artist for over six months by the time it is finished.
Future perfect continuous *be going to*	The artist **is going to have been painting** the mural for over six months by the time it is finished.	The mural **is going to have been being painted** by the artist for over six months by the time it is finished.

WORK SHEET 19

Verb Tense

Verbs in the past continuous tense are used to indicate that a longer action in the past was interrupted.

I Put the verbs into the correct past continuous form.

1 When I phoned my friends, they (play) cricket.

____

2 Yesterday at six I (prepare) dinner.

____

3 The children (play) in the garden when it suddenly began to rain.

____

4 I (practice) the guitar when my father came home.

____

5 We (not/cycle) today.

____

6 While Bhaskar (work) in his room, his friends (swim) in the pool.

____

7 I tried to tell them the truth but they (listen/not).

____

8 What (you/do) yesterday?

____

9 Most of the time we (study) in the class.

____

10 We (eat) dinner and (discuss) our holiday plans.

____

WORK SHEET 20

Verb Tense

The future continuous tense indicates action at a specific point in time in the future.

I Make the following positive future continuous sentences.

At 3 o'clock tomorrow ...

1 I (work) in my office.

____

2 You (lie) on the bed.

____

3 He (wait) for the bus.

____

4 She (shop) for new clothes.

____

5 It (rain).

____

6 We (get) ready to play.

____

7 They (meet) their friends.

____

8 She (study) for the exam.

____

9 He (exercise) at the gym.

____

10 I (sleep).

____

Verb Tense

We use the future tenses when there is no plan or decision to do something.

I Complete the sentences with either the future perfect tense or the future perfect continuous tense.

1 By 2011 we __________ (live) in Delhi for eight years.

2 He __________ (write) an essay by the end of the week.

3 He __________ (read) this book for three months by the end of this week.

4 __________ (finish, you) your homework by the next week?

5 We __________ (married, be) a year on 25th June.

6 Ted __________ (have) his car for over six months by next Monday.

7 By the time I finally finish studying, I __________ (be) a student for over ten years.

8 Do you suppose you __________ (finish) by tonight?

9 By the time he gets here, we __________ (wait) for him for an hour.

10 Everything __________ (make) spotless in time for the party.

Verb Tense

When speaking in the past perfect continuous tense, we often contract the subject and the verb. For example: **I had been** becomes **I'd been**.

I Complete the sentences by putting the verbs into the correct form.

1 By the end of the week I (work) here for four months.

____

2 By the end of this month we (live) together for six years.

____

3 By the end of the term she (study) for nine years.

____

4 By midnight we (play) this computer game for forty-eight hours.

____

5 She (talk) on the phone for the last couple of hours.

____

6 They (look for) me all night long.

____

7 He (play) soccer all day long.

____

8 You (watch) TV all the time.

____

9 He (not/sleep) all morning.

____

10 (wait/they) for two hours?

____

Clauses

A clause is a group of words with a subject and verb.

➔ Shankar and Gayatri went shopping.

➔ The singer won a prize.

There are two kinds of clauses:

Principal clause

The principal clause consists of one main idea. It is also known as the main clause.

➔ Shankar loves shopping.

➔ Birds fly home at sunset.

Clauses

Subordinate clause

A subordinate clause says more about the main idea in the principal clause. The subordinate clause is connected to the principal clause by a conjunction or a relative pronoun. The subordinate clause can be placed at the beginning, middle or at the end of a sentence.

➩ Shankar loves shopping *when he has free time.*

➩ *When the sun sets,* I will go for a walk.

➩ If you call me *when you get home,* I will come over.

Subordinate clauses are linked to the principal clause by conjunctions or relative pronouns. The relative pronouns we use to join clauses include **who** and **whom** when we are talking about people and **which** and **that** when talking about things.

➩ That is the girl *who punched my face.*

➩ This is the house *that my mother grew up in.*

Subordinate clauses can do the work of adverbs, nouns and adjectives.

- **Noun clauses:** Noun clauses do the work of nouns. They usually tell us what someone is doing, saying or feeling.

➩ He asked me *if I loved cheese.*

- **Adverbial clauses:** Adverbial clauses do the work of adverbs and tell us more about the verb.

➩ I'll do laundry *when I run out of clothes.*

- **Adjectival clauses:** Adjectival clauses do the work of adjectives and tell us more about people and things.

➩ The planet, *which has just been discovered,* may contain life.

Clauses

I Fill in the blanks with the correct adverbial clause.

1 Fred looks ______________ something is wrong.

2 The wedding party danced ______________ the music played.

3 Kaveri goes swimming ______________ her illness.

4 ______________ I looked, I found biscuit crumbs.

5 This region is called the valley of flowers ______________ of the sheer number of flowers that blossom here.

6 ______________ ploughing the field, the farmer struck oil.

7 Devdas can't attend the meeting ______________ he finds socks.

8 ______________ the kebabs started cooking, everyone developed an appetite.

9 ______________ pandas mostly eat bamboo, they also east shoots and leaves.

10 Seat belts were introduced ______________ traffic fatalities would reduce.

11 ______________ his parents disapprove, he refuses to cut his hair.

12 ______________ running, grizzly bears are capable of attaining a speed of 70 kilometres an hour.

Clauses

I Change each of the sentences given below into an adjectival clause modifying the words in bold.

1 Let me introduce you to **my dog**. Her name is Cezane.

____

2 **The book** changed my life. It is full of useful advice about heartbreak.

____

3 **Mother Goose nursery rhymes** are rarely terribly profound. Most children are familiar with them.

____

4 **The Jolly Jelly** is my favourite restaurant. I eat there every day.

____

5 We spoke to **a man**. He was German.

____

6 I have lost **the piggy bank**. You had bought it for my birthday.

____

7 He laughs at **my mother's jokes**. They are never funny.

____

8 **The children** were playing. I saw them.

____

9 She lost **the hat**. She had bought it last week.

____

10 I spoke to **that man**. He said he would call me today.

____

WORK SHEET 25

Clauses

Relative clauses provide important information to define or identify the person or thing being talked about.

I Create main clauses of your own to make full sentences with the subordinate clauses given below:

1 Since he had no socks

____

2 If I had a spoon

____

3 Which you were probably saving

____

4 When you came home late

____

5 Because I said so

____

6 Whose house it was in

____

7 Although she did visit once

____

8 Since he arrived

____

9 Shocked by the news

____

10 After work today

____

Clauses

A subordinate clause cannot stand alone without a main clause because it does not provide a complete thought.

I. In each of the following sentences, identify the principal and subordinate clauses.

1 Garfield and I don't like Mondays.

2 I do my homework before I go to bed.

3 I need a new pair of shoes.

4 Will there be pizza later?

5 Because the exam was difficult, none of the students did well.

6 You must call me as soon as you reach.

7 I don't know yet whether I will be in tomorrow.

8 This sentence is a principal clause.

9 I might have food poisoning if you cook dinner.

10 How much money have you got?

11 I am having a lot of trouble passing my driving test.

12 My dog, who loves pizzas, eats them under the kitchen table, where he chews with great enthusiasm.

LESSON 10

Sentences

A sentence is a group of words that conveys meaning when put together.

Simple Sentences

A simple sentence is also an independent clause. It contains a subject and a verb and it expresses a complete thought. In the following simple sentences, subjects are in **bold**, and verbs are in *italics*:

- Some **students** *like* to study in the evenings.
- **Juan** and **Arturo** *play* cricket every afternoon.
- **I** *go* to the library and *study* every day.

Compound Sentences

A compound sentence contains two independent clauses joined by coordinators like for, and, nor, but, or, yet and so. In the following sentences, subjects are in **bold**, verbs are in *italics* and coordinators are ***bold*** and ***italic***.

- **I** *tried* to speak Spanish, ***and*** my **friend** *tried* to speak English.
- **Pooja** *played* football, ***so*** **Maria** *went* shopping.
- **Vishal** *played* football, ***for*** **Maria** *went* shopping.

The above are compound sentences. Each sentence contains two independent clauses and is joined by a coordinator with a comma preceding it. Note how the coordinators can change the relationship between the clauses. Sentences 2 and 3 are similar except for the coordinators.

In sentence 2, which action occurred first? Obviously, **Pooja played football** first, and as a consequence, **Maria went shopping.** In sentence 2, **Maria went shopping** first. In sentence 3, **Vishal played football** because, possibly, he didn't have anything else to do, *for* or *because* **Maria went shopping.**

Complex Sentences

A complex sentence has an independent clause joined by one or more dependent clauses. A complex sentence **always** has a subordinator such as because, since, after, although or when or a relative

Sentences

pronoun such as that, who, or which. In the following complex sentences, subjects are in **bold**, verbs are in *italics* and the subordinators are **bold** and ***italic***.

- ***When*** **he** *handed* in his homework, **he** *forgot* to give the teacher the last page.
- The **students** *are studying* ***because*** **they** *have* an exam tomorrow.
- **Rohan** and **I** *went* to the movies ***after*** **we** *finished* dancing.

Types of sentences	What it does	Examples
Simple sentences	State one thought.	Sports cars have great speed. I love spicy food.
Compound sentences connected with **and, but, or**	Connect equal ideas, add a thought, or take exception.	Sports cars are fast, ***and*** many people love that about them. I love spicy food, ***but*** not everyone appreciates it.
Complex sentences connected with	Combine main clauses with one or more dependent clauses	
because	Explains the reason for the subsequent clause.	Babies are finicky eaters ***because*** they have very sensitive stomachs.
since	Use when showing time.	I've been raising cats ***since*** I was eight years old. 
although, even though	Qualify a thought: despite what is stated in the dependent clause, the main clause remains true.	***Although*** he can be downright unbearable at times, he is a good friend. I will always eat spicy food **even though** they can sometimes destroy my stomach.

Sentences

Types of sentences	What it does	Examples
Complex sentences connected with **if**		
... then	Establishes a condition and explains what would happen as a result.	***If*** you abuse a pet, ***then*** it will not be affectionate towards you.
as if	Introduces an idea that explains the main clause	Beowulf scowled, ***as if*** he were really angry.
so that, so	Explains the reason for the action of the main clause	Mail the letter now, ***so that*** it will arrive on time.

Sentences

A complex sentence always has a subordinator.

I Identify the following sentences as simple, complex or compound. The key is to find the subjects and verbs first.

1 The teacher walked into the classroom, greeted the students, and took attendance.

a simple *b* compound *c* complex

2 I played football while my mother went shopping.

a simple *b* compound *c* complex

3 We played video games, yet Vijay played football.

a simple *b* compound *c* complex

4 Although Brazil has the better football team, it lost.

a simple *b* compound *c* complex

5 The island was filled with many roads winding through the thick underbrush, a small lake, and many stray dogs.

a simple *b* compound *c* complex

6 Revathi passed the exam because she had studied hard and understood the material.

a simple *b* compound *c* complex

7 We visited the museum before it burned down.

a simple *b* compound *c* complex

8 There are some dreams that cannot die.

a simple *b* compound *c* complex

9 We waited for the train, but the train was late.

a simple *b* compound *c* complex

10 My friend invited me to her wedding, but I do not want to go.

a simple *b* compound *c* complex

WORK SHEET 28

Sentences

A compound sentence is a sentence with two or more subjects joined by a conjunction.

I Combine the following simple sentences into complex sentences.

1 His name is Sachin.
He's a famous professional sportsperson.
He's a cricket player.

____

____

2 He has a large house in the suburbs.
He lives in a flat in the city.

____

____

3 He often travels around the world.
He works in different cities.
He travels by airplane.

____

____

4 He usually sleeps in the train.
He stays late in the office.

____

____

5 He is an excellent writer.
Fans love his stories.
His books sell well.

____

____

Sentences

Connectors like **and**, **but** and **or** can turn simple sentences into complex or compound sentenes.

I Combine the following simple sentences into complex sentences.

1 Every week I play squash.
I play at a nearby sports complex.
The game is usually an hour long.

____

____

2 Glover Stadium is old.
Glover Stadium doesn't have enough seats for all the fans.

____

____

3 Scientists are working on a cure for the common cold.
I think it will be remarkable when they find one.

____

____

4 The fans are unhappy about the concert ticket prices.
The fans love the band.

____

____

5 There is a species of Monarch butterflies.
They migrate to Mexico every year.
They are guided by instinct.

____

____

Punctuation

If sentences are a means of conveying information, punctuation is a way of clarifying that information and imbuing it with personality.

Full stop

We use full stops to denote the end of a sentence.

➩ I am scared of small cats.

But if the last word in the sentence ends in a full stop, do not follow it with another full stop.

➩ Please shop and cook. I will clean up after dinner.

Comma

We use commas to separate words or word groups of three or more.

➩ I need to pick up some tomatoes, beans and cake.

We also use commas to separate parts of a date and specific places.

➩ Mary met her husband on 2 December 1983, in Mill Valley, California.

We use commas for large numbers.

➩ 1,000

➩ 7,86,432

➩ $64,050.75

LESSON 11

Punctuation

Question mark

These are used to indicate a direct question.

- What is your name?

Exclamation mark

Exclamation marks are used to show emphasis or surprise.

- Great work!

Ellipses

Ellipses are useful when you're quoting material and you want to omit some words.

The original sentence from Lincoln's Gettysburg Address is as follows:

- "Four score and seven years ago our fathers brought forth, upon this continent, a new nation, conceived in liberty, and dedicated to the proposition that all men are created equal."

This can be rewritten using ellipses:

- "Four score and seven years ago our fathers brought forth ... a new nation, conceived in liberty ..."

Colon

A colon really does only one thing: it introduces. It can introduce just about anything: a word, a phrase, a sentence, a quotation or a list.

- Vivek has only one thing on his mind: dinosaurs.
- There are three ways you can make a good impression on your customers:

  a. Dress appropriately.

  b. Be prompt.

  c. Be courteous.

LESSON 11

Punctuation

Semicolon

A semicolon is used in place of a full stop to separate two sentences usually where the conjunction has been left out.

- Call me tomorrow; I may be free then.

Apostrophe

We use apostrophes with contractions. They are also used to show possession.

- The terminator said he'll be back.
- This is Sarah's hat.

Quotes

Quotation marks are used to mark off material that represents quoted or spoken language. We also use quotes to mark the titles of short stories, poems and articles.

- My father always said, "Be careful what you wish for."
- What do you think of Robert Frost's poem "Design"?

LESSON 11

Punctuation

Dash

Dashes are often used to indicate a break in thought or a shift in tone. They also indicate interruptions in speech.

- "How many times have I asked you not to —" Jason suddenly stopped.
- "Not to do what?" I prompted.
- "Not to — Oh no, I forget!"

Hyphen

Hyphens should not be confused with a dash, which is longer. Hyphens are used to join compound words.

- pre-school
- mother-in-law

They are also used to make compound modifiers.

- a blue-eyed boy
- a well-known actor

Brackets

Brackets are used to provide information that may or may not be relevant to the situation.

- I will meet Varun (who went to school with me).
- Please read the report (attached to this e-mail).

Full stops go inside the brackets only if an entire sentence is inside the brackets.

- Please read the report. (I've attached it to this e-mail.)

WORK SHEET 30

Punctuation

Exclamation marks indicate strong emotion. Never use more than one exclamation mark in the sentence.

I Choose the correct answer based on the punctuation required for the sentence.

1 I won't be home until after ____________ call until then.

a 2:30, don't *b* 1:30; don't *c* 2:00: don't

2 I was late for my ____________ I missed the bus.

a class; because *b* class because, *c* class because

3 This is what you'll need ____________ a notebook, a box of crayons and some paper.

a to buy, *b* to buy: *c* to buy;

4 ____________ I'm not sure I believe that.

a Really— *b* Really: *c* Really?

5 He's lived in ____________.

a San Francisco, California, Portland, Oregon and Dallas, Texas

b San Francisco, California. Portland, Oregon. and Dallas, Texas

c San Francisco, California; Portland, Oregon; and Dallas, Texas

6 You'll need to talk to ____________ about setting up an appointment.

a Angela—she's Dr Connor's secretary—

b Angela, she's Dr Connor's secretary,

c Angela. She's Dr Connor's secretary

7 ____________ is much smaller than Delhi.

a Kolkata: the capital of West Bengal

b Kolkata (the capital of West Bengal)

c Kolkata, the capital of West Bengal;

Punctuation

Never use a comma to separate a verb or preposition from its subject in a sentence.

I The following passage is from Mark Twain's *The Adventures of Tom Sawyer*. Unfortunately, there are no punctuation marks. Rewrite the passage with the correct punctuation and make the story readable.

Tip: Pay close attention to the verbs used to indicate emphasis.

Tom No answer Tom No answer What's gone with that boy I wonder You Tom No answer The old lady

___

pulled her spectacles down and looked over them about the room then she put them up and looked

___

out under them She seldom or never looked through them for so small a thing as a boy they were her

___

state pair the pride of her heart and were built for style not service she could have seen through a

___

pair of stove-lids just as well She looked perplexed for a moment, and then said, not fiercely, but still

___

loud enough for the furniture to hear Well, I lay if I get hold of you I'll She did not finish, for by this

___

time she was bending down and punching under the bed with the broom, and so she needed breath

___

to punctuate the punches with She resurrected nothing but the cat I never did see the beat of that

___

boy She went to the open door and stood in it and looked out among the tomato vines and "jimpson"

___

weeds that constituted the garden. No Tom. So she lifted up her voice at an angle calculated for

___

distance and shouted Tom

___

LESSON 12

Direct and Indirect Speech

Saying **exactly** what someone has said is called direct speech (sometimes called quoted speech). Here what a person says appears within quotation marks ("...") and should be exactly what was said:

- She said, "Today's lesson is on presentations."

or

- "Today's lesson is on presentations," she said.

Indirect speech (sometimes called reported speech) doesn't use quotation marks to enclose what the person said and it doesn't have to be word for word.

Tense Change

When reporting speech, the tense usually changes. This is because when we use reported speech, we are usually talking about a time in the past (because obviously the person who spoke originally spoke in the past). The verbs, therefore, usually have to be in the past too.

- "I'm going to the cinema", he said. (**Direct speech**)
- He said that he was going to the cinema. (**Indirect speech**)

Direct and Indirect Speech

In reported speech, all statements are in the past tense as the event has already occured.

Direct speech	Indirect speech
Present simple She said, "It's cold."	**Past simple** She said that it was cold.
Present continuous She said, "I'm studying English online."	**Past continuous** She said that she was studying English online.
Present perfect simple She said, "I've been using the internet since 1999."	**Past perfect simple** She said that she had been using the internet since 1999.
Present perfect continuous She said, "I've been playing tennis for seven years."	**Past perfect continuous** She said that she had been playing tennis for seven years.
Past simple She said, "I checked my e-mail yesterday."	**Past perfect** She said that she had checked her e-mail the previous day.
Past continuous She said, "I was teaching earlier."	**Past perfect continuous** She said that she had been teaching earlier.
Past perfect She said, "The lesson had already started when he arrived."	**Past perfect** *No change in tense*. She said that the lesson had already started when he arrived.
Past perfect continuous She said, "I'd already been teaching for five minutes."	**Past perfect continuous** *No change in tense*. She said that she'd already been teaching for five minutes.

Direct and Indirect Speech

Some verb forms also change at times:

Direct speech	Indirect speech
will She said, "I'll buy my textbooks tomorrow."	**would** She said that she would buy her textbooks the following day.
can She said, "I can learn English online."	**could** She said that she could learn English online.
must She said, "I must have a computer to learn English online."	**had to** She said that she had to have a computer to learn English online.
shall She said, "What shall we study today?"	**should** She asked what we should study that day.
may She said, "May I open a new browser?"	**might** She asked if she might open a new browser.

WORK SHEET 32

Direct and Indirect Speech

Indirect speech is almost always written in the past tense.

I Rewrite the following sentences in indirect (reported) speech.

1 He said, "I have eaten my lunch."

____

2 She said, "I am studying engineering at the university."

____

3 The teacher said to the class, "Pay attention."

____

4 My mother said to me, "Buy some cake for me."

____

5 My father said to me, "Don't waste your money."

____

6 She asked me, "Where is the hospital?"

____

7 My friend said to me. "Don't be late tomorrow."

____

8 He asked me, "When will the train reach?"

____

9 His teacher said to him, "Try to do it by yourself."

____

10 She asked me, "What are your favourite sports?"

____

Direct and Indirect Speech

Direct speech is often indicated by the use of quote marks (" ").

I Circle all the instances of direct speech and underline all the reported speech.

The Canterville Ghost

By Oscar Wilde

Chapter VI

About ten minutes later, the bell rang for dinner, and, as Virginia did not come down, Mrs Otis sent up one of the servants. After a little time he returned and said that he could not find Miss Virginia anywhere. So, the whole family started looking for her.

The hours passed, but they could find no trace of Virginia. So, after dinner, Mr Otis ordered them all to bed, saying that nothing more could be done that night, and that he would contact Scotland Yard in the morning. Just when everybody was about to leave the dining-room, the clock struck midnight, and when the last stroke sounded, a secret door opened in the wall and in that door stood Virginia with a little box in her hand. Everybody ran up to her.

"Good heavens! child, where have you been?" said Mr Otis, rather angrily, as he thought she had been playing a trick on them.

"Papa," said Virginia quietly, "I have been with the ghost. He is dead, and you must come and see him. He had been very nasty, but he was really sorry for all that he had done, and he gave me this box of beautiful jewels before he died."

Then she led the others down a narrow secret corridor to a little low room. There the family found the skeleton of Sir Simon, who had been starved to death by his wife's brothers. Virginia knelt down beside the skeleton, and, folding her little hands together, began to pray silently.

Meanwhile, one of the twins was looking out of the window in the little room and suddenly said, "Look! The old almond tree has blossoms."

"Then God has forgiven him," said Virginia and stood up.

Direct and Indirect Speech

There is no change in tense when writing past perfect tense in indirect speech.

I Rewrite the following as indirect speech.

1 I said," This man is not reliable."

2 She said to me, "Your singing is making the children cry."

3 You said, "My bike skidded to a halt."

4 He said, "I have done amazingly well today."

5 We said, "We watched a terrible movie."

6 She said, "I may need some medical help soon."

7 You said to me, "You can do this ridiculously easy task."

8 I said, "I shall certainly take care of all eventualities."

9 He said, "I will teach him a lesson to remember me by."

10 They said, "We have put up an unstable building."

LESSON 13

Homophones and Homonyms

A **homophone** is a word that is pronounced the same as another word but differs in meaning.

➩ board and bored

A **homonym** is a word that has the same spelling and the same pronunciation as another word but differs in meaning.

➩ rose: the flower and the past tense of **to rise**

A homograph is a word that is spelt the same but not pronounced the same as another word. The words also differ in meaning.

➩ read: simple past and read simple present

The following sentences illustrate how confusing (and amusing) homophones, homonyms and homographs can be.

➩ The bandage was wound around the wound.

The soldier decided to desert his dessert in the desert.

➩ Upon seeing the tear in the painting, I shed a tear.

➩ The dump was so full that it had to refuse more refuse.

➩ We were too close to the door to close it.

LESSON 13

Homophones and Homonyms

Effect vs Affect

One of the most common errors in the English language is the misuse of **effect** and **affect** because of how similiar sounding these words are.

Affect may mean to alter or change the feelings of someone or something. It may also mean, in a broader sense, to change or affect someone or something in any way.

➩ The song affected him so deeply he could not stop dancing.

The word effect, in contrast, refers to the result of something, the power something might have to get that result, or a phenomenon in the world.

➩ The effect of the song on him was so profound that he danced until his feet fell off.

Most of the time, effect is a noun and affect is a verb.

If you are unsure, try substituting a different verb for **affect** and see if it works.

Many animals will be affected by climate change.

Many animals will be ~~affected~~ eaten by climate change.

Since **eaten** does work, clearly a noun is not required here, and only the verb **affect** is applicable.

A sentence demonstrating the various uses of these two words might be:

➩ Although music seemed to affect him deeply, its true effects would not be known until after the wine—which had affected his judgement—wore off.

WORK SHEET 35

Homophones and Homonyms

A homophone is a word that is pronounced the same as another word but has a different meaning.

I Put the correct homophone in the sentence.

1 *allowed, aloud*

The teacher told us to read ____________ from the book.

Jack's mother ____________ him to sell the family cow.

2 *berth, birth*

I slept in the lower ____________ in the train.

Our neighbour gave ____________ to a baby girl.

3 *board, bored*

He nailed a ____________ to hide the broken window.

Whenever I get ____________, I watch TV.

4 *blew, blue*

The wind ____________ his toupee off.

The sky is a deep colour of ____________ today.

5 *ceiling, sealing*

This tape is much better for ____________ packages than the other one.

It took him about four hours to fix the hole in the ____________.

Homophones and Homonyms

A homonym is a word that shares the same spelling and pronunciation as another word, but has a different meaning.

I The following poem was run through an electronic spellchecker and it found no mistakes. This is because the poem uses homophones.

Can you rewrite the poem using the correct words?

An Owed to the Spelling Checker

by Jerrold H. Zar

I have a spelling checker.
It came with my PC.
It plane lee marks four my revue
Miss steaks aye can knot sea.

Eye ran this poem threw it,
Your sure reel glad two no.
Its vary polished in it's weigh,
My checker tolled me sew.

A checker is a bless sing,
It freeze yew lodes of thyme.
It helps me right awl stiles two reed,
And aides me when aye rime.

Each frays come posed up on my screen
Eye trussed to bee a joule
The checker poured o'er every word
To cheque sum spelling rule.

WORK SHEET 37

Homophones and Homonyms

A homograph is a word that is spelt the same as another word, but differs in pronunciation and meaning.

Be fore a veiling checkers
Hour spelling mite decline,
And if were lacks or have a laps,
We wood be maid to wine.

Butt now bee cause my spelling
Is checked with such grate flare,
Their are know faults with in my cite,
Of none eye am a wear.

Now spelling does knot phase me,
It does knot bring a tier.
My pay purrs awl due glad den
With wrapped words fare to hear.

To rite with care is quite a feet
Of witch won should be proud.
And wee mussed dew the best wee can,
Sew flaw's are knot aloud.

Sow ewe can sea why aye dew prays
Such soft ware for pea seas,
And why I brake in two averse
By righting wants too pleas.

Revision 1

I Identify the parts of speech in bold (verbs, nouns, adjectives, adverbs, pronouns, prepositions, conjunctions).

1 I bought a **beautiful** dress the other day. ______________

2 What did **she** ask you to do? ______________

3 I left my shoes **under** the kitchen table. ______________

4 If we finish our work **quickly**, we can go play. ______________

5 On Mondays I **work** from nine to five. ______________

6 I want to go to a **college** in a big city. ______________

7 I'm sure I have **met** your mother before. ______________

8 **Well**, I don't think I will be here to answer the door. ______________

9 I knocked on the door **but** nobody answered. ______________

10 **After** lunch let's go out for a coffee. ______________

11 **Always** remember that you're unique, just like everyone else. ______________

12 The baby is using her **unbreakable** toy to break other toys. ______________

13 Ted said, "I **pretend** to work; they pretend to pay me." ______________

14 Ravi told me a joke **about** a pencil that was pointless. ______________

II Fill in the blanks. Identify the parts of speech used.

1 ______________ the answer is correct, give yourself one point. ______________

2 They ______________ had time to finish their lunch before the taxi arrived. ______________

3 These ______________ flowers look lovely in the garden. ______________

Revision 1

4 ______________ ! I could not believe how much that hurt. ______________

5 Sayoni carried the gifts ______________ the room. ______________

6 ______________ of these shirts could be folded a little more neatly. ______________

7 My sister's ______________ had to be towed to the mechanic yesterday. ______________

8 The broken computer was ______________ by my nephew in minutes. ______________

9 We ______________ a colourful poster from the stationery shop. ______________

10 Tall, dark and ______________, Batman makes his presence known immediately. ______________

11 I have not spoken to the principal ______________ this yet. ______________

12 Neither of ______________ had been invited to the party. ______________

13 Yes, I would love to be there, ______________ I have school tomorrow. ______________

14 Rita was elected as our next ______________. ______________

15 The police officers had trouble chasing the ______________ thief. ______________

16 All of the guests ______________ approached the birthday boy. ______________

17 I could ______________ do much with that cracked table. ______________

18 Caleb thanked the ______________ for all their help. ______________

19 Most of the people wanted to see the ______________ who had entered the building. ______________

20 The ambulance was carefully ______________ by the experienced driver. ______________

Revision 1

III Fill in the blanks with the correct conjunction.

1 Do you think this is something ____________ can be fixed?

a who *b* when *c* that

2 Don't go out ____________ you've showered.

a as *b* until *c* while

3 Make sure you bring in the clothes ____________ it starts to rain.

a after *b* before *c* for

4 ____________ I had known how much it would hurt him, I wouldn't have done it.

a Whether *b* When *c* If

5 It's no surprise ____________ he failed the exam.

a why *b* until *c* where

6 ____________ it gets dark, come inside.

a While *b* As soon as *c* Whether

7 My friend Ekrem, ____________ lives in Turkey, visits me on my birthday.

a whose *b* who *c* that

8 She's ____________ an unpleasant woman ____________ nobody wants to work with her.

a such ... that *b* such ... as *c* so ... that

9 ____________ we're broke, we can't buy nice things.

a Since *b* While *c* Now

10 He fell asleep ____________ watching the movie.

a while *b* since *c* when

Revision 1

IV Fill in the blanks with the correct relative pronoun.

1 I helped the man ______________ car had broken down outside my house.

2 The unruly students ______________ kept shouting were not from my school.

3 What did you do with the money ______________ I lent you?

4 That's Peter, ______________ just arrived.

5 That's the car ______________ was broken into.

Paragraph Writing

The purpose of a paragraph is to express **one** point, idea or opinion.

This main idea is expressed through three sections of a paragraph:

1. Opening: Introduce your idea.
2. Middle: Explain your idea.
3. End: Make your point again and then transition to the next paragraph.

Here is a paragraph taken from an essay on various strategies required for an overall improvement of student performance:

Students require more recreational time in order to better focus on lessons in class. In fact, studies have shown that students who enjoy a break time of more than forty-five minutes consistently score better on tests immediately following the recess period. Clinical analysis further suggests that physical exercise greatly improves the ability to focus on academic materials. Longer periods of recess are required to allow students the best possible chances of success in their studies. Clearly, physical exercise is just one of the necessary ingredients for improving student scores on standardised tests.

There are four types of sentences used to construct a paragraph:

1. Topic Sentence

This is the sentence that states your idea, point or opinion. It forms the opening section of the paragraph. This sentence should use a strong verb and make a bold statement.

➾ Students require more recreational time in order to better focus on lessons in class.

Note: Notice the strong verb **require**, which acts like a call to action. A less strong form of this sentence might be: *I think students probably need more recreational time...*

2. Supporting Sentences

Supporting sentences provide explanations and support for the topic sentence (main idea) of your paragraph. These form part of the middle section of the paragraph.

➾ In fact, studies have shown that students who enjoy a break time of more than forty-five minutes consistently score better on tests immediately following the recess period. Clinical analysis further suggests that physical exercise greatly improves the ability to focus on academic materials.

Paragraph Writing

Note: Supporting sentences provide the evidence for your topic sentence. Supporting sentences that include facts, statistics and reasoning are much more convincing than simply stating opinions.

3. Concluding Sentence

The concluding sentence restates the main idea (found in your topic sentence) and reinforces the point or opinion. This is part of the end section of the paragraph.

⇨ Longer periods of recess are clearly required to allow students the best possible chances of success in their studies.

Note: Concluding sentences **repeat** the main idea of your paragraph in different words.

4. Transitional Sentence

The transitional sentence prepares the reader for the following paragraph, if there is one. This is also part of the end section of the paragraph.

⇨ Clearly, physical exercise is just one of the necessary ingredients for improving student scores on standardised tests.

Note: Transitional sentences should help readers logically understand the connection between your current main idea, point or opinion and the main idea of your next paragraph. In this instance, the phrase, just one of the necessary ingredients ..., prepares the reader for the next paragraph, which will discuss another necessary ingredient for success.

Paragraphs should contain sentences that convey ideas concisely and directly.

Descriptive Paragraphs

One of the most common types of paragraphs is a descriptive paragraph. A descriptive paragraph aims to reveal or expand a subject through carefully selected details. Since the purpose of the paragraph is to describe, it does not usually contain arguments, explanations or narrative. Instead they rely on adjective and adverbs to create tone.

LESSON 14

Paragraph Writing

Given below is a list of points that we could include in a descriptive paragraph about New York City.

- New York City is in the United States.
- New York City is located in New York State.
- It borders on the Atlantic Ocean.
- It was founded in 1625 as "New Amsterdam".
- It is important for commerce.
- Wall Street is located in New York City.
- It has many national and international banks.
- It has many important skyscrapers.
- Many tourists visit it.
- It is an expensive place to live.
- The Empire State Building is in New York City.

Given below is a descriptive paragraph based on these points. Note how the three sections of a paragraph are used here.

Opening

[Located in New York State, New York City is one of the largest cities in the world.] Its sprawling size and numerous tourist attractions make it a popular and expensive place to live. Founded in 1625 by Dutch settlers, it was originally called "New Amsterdam". Bordering the Atlantic Ocean, New York City was an emerging hub for commerce. It now boasts of several national and international banks, many of them located in famous skyscrapers like the Empire State Building. [Many of us are familiar with the diorama of New York City through the many movies and books set there.]

End section

Paragraph Writing

I Read the information below about Batman.

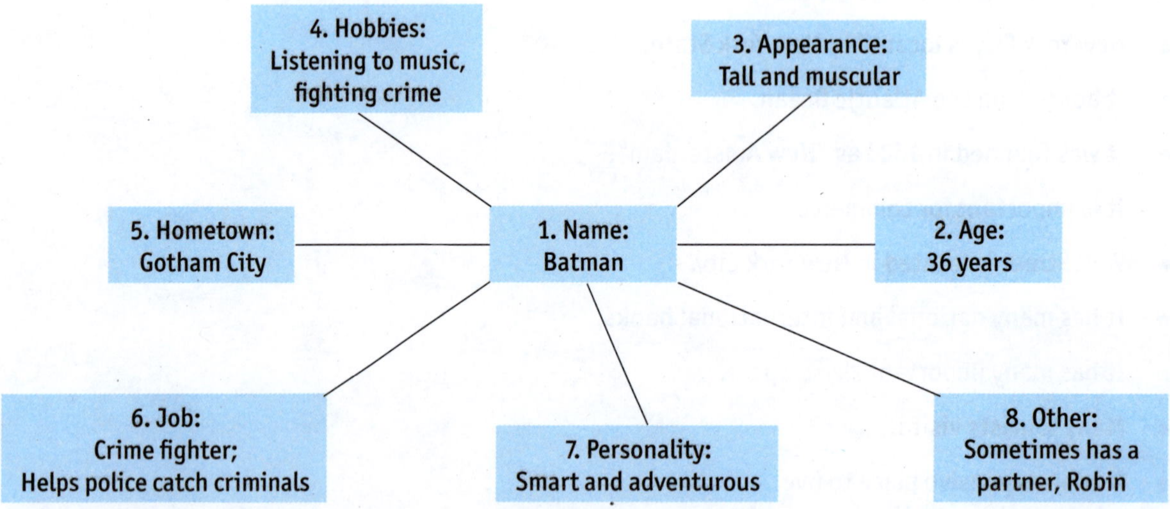

II Now write the information as sentences. The first one has been done for you.

1 His name is Batman.

2 ______________________________

3 ______________________________

4 ______________________________

5 ______________________________

6 ______________________________

7 ______________________________

8 ______________________________

Paragraph Writing

III After you have finished, check your writing with a partner. Then rewrite the sentences as one paragraph.

Paragraph Writing

I **Pick a student to write about. Take a few minutes to gather details about the person you pick. Layout the information you have in the word cloud below.**

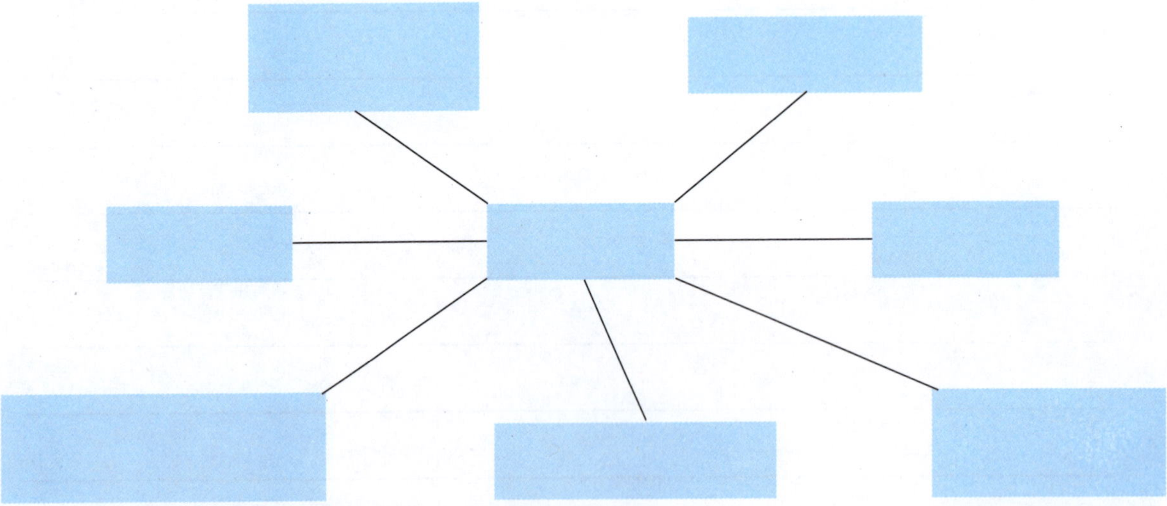

II **Now, write the information as sentences.**

1 ______________________________

2 ______________________________

3 ______________________________

4 ______________________________

5 ______________________________

6 ______________________________

7 ______________________________

8 ______________________________

Paragraph Writing

III Rewrite the sentences as one paragraph.

Paragraph Writing

I **Write a descriptive paragraph on either your journey to school every morning or a visit to the grocery shop. Try to include words that tell you about the sights, sounds and smells that you encounter.**

Informal letter writing

Even in this age of e-mails and text messages, writing a letter is an important skill.

Read the following letter and note the different parts.

27 Crescent Drive
Old Manali Town
Manali
Himachal Pradesh
10th March 2010 — heading

Dear Harish, — salutation

I reached Manali yesterday and I thought I should write this before I forget. It's beautiful here—the days are warm, the nights cool. There are so many stars in the sky. The smog covered skies of Delhi seem far away. I am staying with a few cousins of mine. They have ambitious plans for the upcoming week—fishing, hiking, a drive up to Rohtang Pass, etc. I don't know where the energy for all this will come from, but I'm looking forward to it.
I wish you were here. I trust things are well and you're enjoying yourself at the wedding. — body

Take care, — closing

Sunit — signature

P.S. I forgot to bring my phone with me, and so I might not be able to call you until I return to Delhi. — postscript

Informal letter writing

Six Parts of an Informal Letter

Heading: This is the address and date of the person writing the letter. It is unlikely that someone will remember your address, so it is always a good idea to include it. Remember, this is the address they have to write to for the letter to reach you. The recipient's address is on the envelope.

Salutation: This is a fancy word for greeting. The most common salutation in an informal letter is **Dear ...** .

Body: This is the main part of the letter where you write what you have to say to the person. It can be several paragraphs, and should have a beginning, middle and an end. Start with a greeting and end with a goodbye.

Closing: The closing is the ending to your letter. There are many closing remarks to choose from depending on your relationship with the recipient. Some popular ones are: sincerely, love, best wishes.

Signature: This is an important part of the letter as it identifies the writer. It appears directly under the closing. If you are sure the person will know who you are, just sign your first name. If not, add your last name.

A signature is your personal mark and it should always be written by hand, even if the rest of the letter had been typed.

Postscript: Sometimes when you've finished writing a letter, you remember something else you wanted to say. To avoid having to rewrite the entire letter, you can add a postscript (post=after, script=writing). If the postscript is too long, you might as well write another letter.

Informal letter writing

I Read the following short piece by Justin Plansinis about his cat.

I have a kitty cat. Her name is Miss Cleo. She's a soft, pretty, calico cat that is about ten months old.

She's also the most diabolical, sinister, ferocious feline that I've ever encountered. And I've got the scratches to prove it.

I didn't think having a cat would be very difficult. Cats are fat and lazy, and they tend to do nothing but eat, sleep all day. This is a life that I can relate to, so I thought things would go well.

Enter Cleo.

From the day I got her, this feline has never shut up.

"MEOW MEOW MEOW" — I want to be fed.

"MEOW MEOW MEOW" — I want attention.

"MEOW MEOW MEOW" — I want to play.

"MEOW MEOW MEOW" — Pet me, human slave!

"BITE!!!" — You weren't petting me properly.

Fur Face never seems to be content. Sometimes I think she scratches me just to prove who's the boss.

I tried pawning the cat off on my parents once. My parents have a nice big house with plenty of room for the cat to prowl around in. This ideal situation (for me anyway) was not to last. Turns out that Miss Cleo has a severe personality conflict with Shelby, one of my parents' cats. Shelby and Cleo get into fierce cat fights. This just goes to show that even other cats can't stand Cleo. So Cleo came back to my apartment.

I'm not sure what to do about kitty. So the adventures of Miss Cleo and me will continue. I can't promise that we'll all come out alive.

II What is the tone of the story? Is it positive or negative? Circle the adjectives and try to determine the tone.

Informal letter writing

III **Write a letter to a friend who has not read the story. Imagine you are the writer of this story. Write a letter to your friend who is thinking of getting a cat.**

WORK SHEET 45

Informal letter writing

IV What tenses are used in the piece? Identify the various tenses used by identifying the subject.

simple present ☐ ____________________

present continuous ☐ ____________________

simple past ☐ ____________________

past continuous ☐ ____________________

present perfect ☐ ____________________

present perfect continuous ☐ ____________________

past perfect ☐ ____________________

past perfect continuous ☐ ____________________

simple future ☐ ____________________

Revision 2

The One That Got Away

I Read the passage.

Travellers will only readily undergo hardship if they are travelling towards something, or away from it. So when Franz von Werra started running, he had no idea what he was running into.

He was a Luftwaffe fighter pilot and such men are generally a breed apart. He kept a lion as a pet while in the Luftwaffe and was an ace, a term for fighter pilot who has shot down more than five enemy aircraft.

During a bombing raid over England, he was shot down and captured in September 1940. Barely a month later, he tried to escape but was recaptured. The second time he made a better-planned escape but failed again.

By January the following year, the British had had enough of him and transferred him to Canada, thinking: *now* let him try and escape. But he was made of sterner stuff.

Just after reaching Canada and on their way to a prison camp, he jumped out of the prison train and was on his way. Unfamiliar with the area, he had to walk for several kilometres until he reached a waterfall.

It was the bitterest part of winter in an especially cold land, von Werra did not have provisions and there was no habitation in sight. He walked along the banks of the frozen St Lawrence River along a direction he estimated as nearly south. Thirty kilometres into his walk and on the edge of hypothermia, he crossed the river. He was nearly finished by then but forced himself to press on and ultimately crossed the border into the US.

That country was neutral during that time, so there was some delay while the angry Canadians asked that the fighter pilot be sent back. Meanwhile, an official from the German Embassy helped von Werra get back on the road and into Mexico, from where he travelled through Brazil and Spain to Italy. Back in Germany, von Werra got right back inside a fighter cockpit. Seven months after his return, engine failure succeeded where Allied hunters had failed. He crashed into the North Sea.

Revision 2

II **What finally happened to Franz von Werra? What does it mean that "engine failure succeeded where Allied hunters had failed"?**

III **In what way was von Werra a "breed apart"?**

IV **Pay close attention to the author's use of tenses. What can you spot and what kind of tense are they?**

Revision 2

V Imagine you are von Werra after escaping from the train. Write a letter to your family about your thoughts, the journey, etc. Use a word cloud to develop details.

Revision 3

The Largest Empire

I Read the passage.

The Mongols were a little known tribe squeezed between the present Russia and China in the early thirteenth century. Eighty-eight years later, they ruled the largest empire the world has ever seen. They really went places.

For one, they had horses. Their cavalrymen were swift, agile marksmen. They had tremendous endurance and were willing to learn from defeated enemies.

By the later twelfth century, the Mongols were only one of five warring tribes in what is known now as the Plateau of Mongolia.

Then there emerged Temujin Khan, also called Genghis, who united the tribes and began an unprecedented campaign of conquest across the known world. Reorganizing his army into fixed units and conquering northern China, Temujin's men rode their ponies into Central Asia, Persia, Russia, Belarus, Ukraine and by 1227, when Genghis Khan died, had conquered even the Caucasus Mountains.

His son Ogedei decided to do better: he destroyed the ruling monarchy of China, took over Bulgaria, Azerbaijan and Armenia. Mongol cavalrymen could travel fast and far, nonstop, on horseback: indeed, to their enemies it seemed as if man and horse were a single, unbeatable unit. They also learnt from their enemies how to bombard and siege cities and forts, destroying entire settlements with the people who lived in them, without remorse.

No army has ever advanced as rapidly, as successfully and as mercilessly as the Mongol cavalrymen, armed with light clothes of fur and with bows and arrows.

Revision 3

II What were some of the reasons for the Mongols' success?

III What further changes did Ogedei make?

IV Pay attention to the author's use of punctuation, particularly colons. What effect does it have on you, the reader?

Revision 3

V **Imagine you were one of the mighty Mongol warriors. Write a letter to a friend from the neighbouring tribe. Mention what changes were happening and what you were doing. Write about your new leader, Temujin.**

WORD BANKS Verb Tense

Tenses allow speakers and writers to express exactly what they want to say.

Present Tense Verbs

Tense	Number	1st Person	2nd Person	3rd Person
Simple present	Singular	I **eat** fish.	You **eat** fish.	He/she/it **eats** fish.
	Plural	We **eat** fish.	You **eat** fish.	They **eat** fish.
Present continuous	Singular	I **am eating** fish.	You **are eating** fish.	He/she/it **is eating** fish.
	Plural	We **are eating** fish.	You **are eating** fish.	They **are eating** fish.
Present perfect	Singular	I **have eaten** fish.	You **have eaten** fish.	He/she/it **has eaten** fish.
	Plural	We **have eaten** fish.	You **have eaten** fish.	They **have eaten** fish.
Perfect continuous	Singular	I **have been eating** fish.	You **have been eating** fish.	He/she/it **has been eating** fish.
	Plural	We **have been eating** fish.	You **have been eating** fish.	They **have been eating** fish.

Past Tense Verbs

Tense	Number	1st Person	2nd Person	3rd Person
Simple past	Singular	I **ate** fish.	You **ate** fish.	He/she/it **ate** fish.
	Plural	We **ate** fish.	You **ate** fish.	They **ate** fish.
Past continuous	Singular	I **was eating** fish.	You **were eating** fish.	He/she/it **was eating** fish.
	Plural	We **were eating** fish.	You **were eating** fish.	They **were eating** fish.
Past perfect	Singular	I **had eaten** fish.	You **had eaten** fish.	He/she/it **had eaten** fish.
	Plural	We **had eaten** fish.	You **had eaten** fish.	They **had eaten** fish.
Perfect continuous	Singular	I **had been eating** fish.	You **had been eating** fish.	He/she/it **had been eating** fish.
	Plural	We **had been eating** fish.	You **had been eating** fish.	They **had been eating** fish.

Future Tense Verbs

Tense	Number	1st Person	2nd Person	3rd Person
Simple future	Singular	I **will eat** fish.	You **will eat** fish.	He/she/it **will eat** fish.
	Plural	We **will eat** fish.	You **will eat** fish.	They **will eat** fish.

WORD BANKS Verb Tense

Future continuous	Singular	I **will be eating** fish.	You **will be eating** fish.	He/she/it **will be eating** fish.
	Plural	We **will be eating** fish.	You **will be eating** fish.	They **will be eating** fish.
Future perfect	Singular	I **will have eaten** fish.	You **will have eaten** fish.	He/she/it **will have eaten** fish.
	Plural	We **will have eaten** fish.	You **will have eaten** fish.	They **will have eaten** fish.
Future Perfect continuous	Singular	I **will have been eating** fish.	You **will have been eating** fish.	He/she/it **will have been eating** fish.
	Plural	We **will have been eating** fish.	You **will have been eating** fish.	They **will have been eating** fish.

We can even add other verbs to clarify our meaning.

➩ I ***could*** have been eating fish.

➩ He ***might*** have eaten fish.

➩ They ***should*** be eating fish.

➩ We ***can*** eat fish.

Verbs

Auxiliary verbs are helping verbs. They provide extra information about a sentence, which is not given by the main verb.

List of helping (**auxiliary**) verbs

- am, aren't (only in inversion, as in Aren't I special?), 'm (as in I'm)
- are, aren't, 're (as in you're)
- be
- been
- can, can't
- could, couldn't
- did, didn't
- do, don't
- does, doesn't
- had, hadn't, 'd (➩ She'd gone out.)
- has, hasn't, 's (➩ She's gone out.)
- have, haven't, 've (➩ I've)
- is, isn't, 's (➩ She's back.)
- may, mayn't
- might, mightn't
- must, mustn't
- ought, oughtn't
- shall, shan't
- should, shouldn't
- was, wasn't
- were, weren't
- will, won't, 'll (➩ she'll)
- would, wouldn't, 'd (➩ I'd go out.)

WORD BANKS Verb Tense

Irregular Verbs

One of the more frustrating things about tenses is learning the irregular verbs by heart. As you know, the past tense forms of regular verbs end in **ed** or **d**, however, irregular verbs just need to be learnt.

Infinitive	Past simple	Past participle
be	was/were	been
beat	beat	beaten
become	became	become
begin	began	begun
bend	bent	bent
bet	bet	bet
bite	bit	bitten
blow	blew	blown
break	broke	broken
bring	brought	brought
build	built	built
burst	burst	burst
buy	bought	bought
catch	caught	caught
choose	chose	chosen
come	came	come
cost	cost	cost
cut	cut	cut
deal	dealt	dealt
dig	dug	dug
do	did	done
draw	drew	drawn
drink	drank	drunk
drive	drove	driven
eat	ate	eaten
fall	fell	fallen

Infinitive	Past simple	Past participle
feed	fed	fed
feel	felt	felt
fight	fought	fought
find	found	found
fly	flew	flown
forbid	forbade	forbidden
forget	forgot	forgotten
freeze	froze	frozen
get	got	got
give	gave	given
go	went	gone
grow	grew	grown
hang	hung	hung
have	had	had
hear	heard	heard
hide	hid	hidden
hit	hit	hit
hold	held	held
hurt	hurt	hurt
keep	kept	kept
know	knew	known
lay	laid	laid
lead	led	led
leave	left	left
lend	lent	lent
let	let	let

WORD BANKS Verb Tense

Infinitive	Past simple	Past participle
lie	lay	lain
light	lit	lit
lose	lost	lost
make	made	made
mean	meant	meant
meet	met	met
pay	paid	paid
put	put	put
read	read	read
ride	rode	ridden
ring	rang	rung
rise	rose	risen
run	ran	run
say	said	said
see	saw	seen
seek	sought	sought
sell	sold	sold
send	sent	sent
set	set	set
sew	sewed	sewn/sewed
shake	shook	shaken
shine	shone	shone
shoot	shot	shot
show	showed	shown
shrink	shrank	shrunk
shut	shut	shut
sing	sang	sung
sink	sank	sunk

Infinitive	Past simple	Past participle
sit	sat	sat
sleep	slept	slept
speak	spoke	spoken
spend	spent	spent
split	split	split
spread	spread	spread
spring	sprang	sprung
stand	stood	stood
steal	stole	stolen
stick	stuck	stuck
sting	stung	stung
stink	stank	stunk
strike	struck	struck
swear	swore	sworn
sweep	swept	swept
swim	swam	swum
swing	swung	swung
take	took	taken
teach	taught	taught
tear	tore	torn
tell	told	told
think	thought	thought
throw	threw	thrown
understand	understood	understood
wake	woke	woken
wear	wore	worn
win	won	won
write	wrote	written

WORD BANKS Pronoun

A pronoun is a substitute for a noun. Some pronouns are: **I, me, she, he, her, him, it, you, they** and **them.**

Pronouns	Pronoun as subject	Pronoun as object	Pronoun as possessive adjective	Possessive pronoun	Reflexive pronoun
1st Person Singular	I	me	my	mine	myself
2nd Person Singular	you	you	your	yours	yourself
3rd Person Singular	he she it	him her it	his her it	his hers its	himself herself itself
1st Person Plural	we	us	our	ours	ourselves
2nd Person Plural	you	you	your	yours	yourselves
3rd Person Plural	they	them	their	theirs	themselves

Irregular Plural Nouns

Singural	Plural
alumnus	alumni
cactus	cacti
focus	foci/focuses
fungus	fungi/funguses
nucleus	nuclei
radius	radii
stimulus	stimuli
axis	axes
analysis	analyses
basis	bases
crisis	crises
diagnosis	diagnoses
ellipsis	ellipses
hypothesis	hypotheses
oasis	oases
paralysis	paralyses
parenthesis	parentheses
synthesis	syntheses
synopsis	synopses

Singural	Plural
thesis	theses
appendix	appendices
index	indeces/indexes
matrix	matrices/matrixes
beau	beaux
bureau	bureaus/bureaux
tableau	tableaux/tableaus
child	children
man	men
ox	oxen
woman	women
bacterium	bacteria
corpus	corpora
criterion	criteria
curriculum	curricula
datum	data
genus	genera
medium	media
memorandum	memoranda

Singural	Plural
phenomenon	phenomena
stratum	strata
deer	deer
fish	fish
means	means
offspring	offspring
series	series
sheep	sheep
species	species
foot	feet
goose	geese
tooth	teeth
antenna	antennae/antennas
formula	formulae/formulas
nebula	nebulae
vertebra	vertebrae
vita	vitae
louse	lice
mouse	mice

WORD BANKS Pronoun

Pronouns Vocabulary Word List

A
all
another
any
anybody
anyone
anything

B
both

E
each
either
everybody
everyone
everything

F
few

H
he
her
hers
herself
him
himself
his

I
I
it
its
itself

M
many
me
mine
more
most
much
my
myself

N
neither
no one
nobody
none
nothing

O
one
other
others
our
ours
ourselves

S
several
she
some
somebody
someone
something

T
that
their
theirs
them
themselves
these
they
this
those

U
us

W
we
what
whatever
which
whichever
who
whoever
whom
whomever
whose

Y
you
your
yours
yourself

WORD BANKS Punctuation

' Apostrophe

An apostrophe can show ownership or missing letters (it is – it's). For ownership, the rules are:

Singular owners add: **'s**.

Plural owners not ending in 's' add: **'s**.

Plural owners ending in 's', add: **s'**.

➩ The monkey snapped my car's antenna and stabbed me with it.

( ) Brackets

Brackets contain a piece of additional information put into the main sentence. We can also use commas to do this job.

➩ The baby (when he is hungry) will bite my finger.

: Colon

A colon introduces more information. This information may be a list or a second clause adding information to the first clause.

➩ These animals are not edible: camels, kangaroos and parrots.

, Comma

A comma separates parts of a sentence and can be similar to a pause in speech.

➩ Although nobody is looking at him, the panda is still hiding in the corner.

— Dash

A dash is used in informal writing.

➩ That hat looks great—everyone will love it.

... Ellipsis

Ellipsis is the name for three dots that show the writing is incomplete.

➩ The lion leapt towards the unsuspecting visitor and before you knew it ...

10. Apostrophes

Apostrophes have two functions: to show contractions (**I won't**) and possession (**Shakespeare's tragedy**). They are not used to show the plural of a noun.

My novel's cover contains numerous inaccuracies. ✔	My novels cover contains numerous inaccuracies. ✘
For now, the terrorists threats have not cowed the community. ✘	For now, the terrorists' threats have not cowed the community. ✔

9. Nouns ending in y

Nouns ending in **y** often produce similar confusion with regard to possession. If you want to talk about something belonging to a country, for instance, write **country's**, not **countries.**

8. Conjunction confusion

Conjunctions like *and*, *but* and *for* join independent clauses. Students often use *however*, *therefore*, and *thus* as if they were conjunctions, but they are not. They're adverbs, and can't connect independent clauses—you'll still need a semicolon or period.

I studied for hours but he never opened a book—and we both topped the exam. ✘	I studied for hours but he never opened a book yet we both topped the exam. ✔

It's usually more graceful to place *however*, *therefore*, and similar words not right at the beginning but at some convenient pause later on:

Truth is a good thing; it is not, however, the highest political good.

7. Infamy and notoriety

Infamous is not a fancy way of saying famous. It means the opposite: famously wicked or bad. Gandhi was famous; Hitler was infamous. Likewise, *notoriety* doesn't mean just being widely known—it means being known for being bad

Although cryogenics was introduced over a decade ago, it is only now receiving the notoriety it deserves. ✘	Although cryogenics was introduced over a decade ago, it is only now receiving the attention it deserves. ✔

6. Practice and practise

In many English-speaking countries (UK, Australia, India and Canada) **practice** is the noun, **practise** the verb. However, in the US, the spelling **practice** is more often used for both the noun and the verb.

You need to practise your English. ✔	You need to practice your English. ✔

5. Advice and advise

Advice is a noun and advise is the verb form and you clearly have to use the noun before the adjective.

She gave me very good advise on buying a car. ✘	She gave me very good advice on buying a car. ✔

4. Intents and purposes

Not intensive purposes.

For all intensive purposes, Apple has won the computer wars. ✘	For all intents and purposes, Apple has won the phone wars. ✔

3. Of or Off

People often use these words interchangeably, but each has its own correct usage. It helps to think of it like this: ***Of*** implies belonging to something or coming from. ***Off*** implies to be removed, away from or less. **Dispose of** is an exception.

The car went of the road. ✘	The car went off the road. ✔

2. Principal/principle

Principal is an adjective meaning **foremost** or **most important**, while principle is a noun meaning **guiding idea.**

The Constitution of India lays down the fundamental rights and principals of citizens. ✘	The Constitution of India lays down the fundamental rights and principles of citizens. ✔

1. It's/its

Because apostrophes are used for possession as well as contraction, many students get confused about the distinction between them. Remember that **it's** is a contraction, not a possessive: *It's = it is*. *It*, like other pronouns (*he, his; she, her*) doesn't take an apostrophe to show possession:

The baby howled when I stole it's toy. ✘	The baby howled when I stole its toy. ✔

Who's and *whose* have the same distinction. *Who's* is a contraction of **who is** or, less commonly, **who has. Whose** is the possessive of **who.**

Whose ready to go out tonight? ✘	Who's ready to go out tonight? ✔

WORD BANKS

Homographs

words that are identical with another in spelling but different in meaning.

angle
arms
back
ball
bank
bar
bark
base
bat
bay
beam
bear
beat
bill
bit
blind
block
blow
board
booty
bow
brand
cape
case
cast
change
charge
chop
club
coach
coat
coast
cold
column
corn

count
court
craft
crane
cricket
crop
cross
crow
dock
down
draught
draw
drill
drive
drone
duck
express
fair
fast
felt
file
fill
fine
fire
fit
flag
fleet
float
fold
foot
form
game
gape
grain
grate

grave
ground
gum
hail
hamper
hand
hide
hit
hold
host
iron
jam
jar
joint
jumper
June
just
kid
kind
kite
lap
last
lay
lead
lean
leaves
left
let
letter
lie
lift
light
line
list
litter

lock
log
mail
march
mass
master
match
may
mean
might
mine
mint
mould
mount
nail
nature
note
order
organ
page
palm
pass
patient
peal
plot
plug
pole
port
post
pound
power
private
prune
pupil
race

range
rank
record
rent
rest
rifle
right
ring
rock
roll
rose
round
row
ruler
rung
sack
safe
save
scale
scales
seal
season
shed
sheet
sign
sink
smoke
soil
sound
sow
speaker
spell
spoke
spring
squash

staff
stage
stall
stand
star
state
steer
stern
stick
stock
stole
strike
stud
stump
suit
swallow
swift
table
tear
temper
tile
till
top
train
trip
tumbler
turn
vote
wake
watch
wave
well
wind
work
yawn

WORD BANKS Homophones

ail / ale
air / heir
aisle / isle / I'll
allowed / aloud
alter / altar
arc / ark
arms / alms
ascent / assent
ate / eight
aunt / aren't
awe / or / oar / ore
bail / bale
bald / bawled
bare / bear
bark / barque
barren / baron
base / bass
be / bee
beach / beech
been / bean
beer / bier
bell / belle
berry / bury
birth / berth
bite / bight
blew / blue
boar / bore
board / bored
boarder / border
bold / bowled
born / borne
bough / bow
bow / beau
boy / buoy
braid / brayed
braise / brays
brake / break
bread / bred
brews / bruise
bridal / bridle
but / butt
buy / by / bye
cannon / canon

canvas / canvass
capital / capitol
carrot / carat
cast / caste
caw / core / corps
cede / seed
ceiling / sealing
cellar / seller
cent / scent / sent
centred / scented
cents / scents / sense
cereal / serial
cheap / cheep
check / cheque
chews / choose
choral / coral
cite / sight / site
clause / claws
coarse / course
coat / cote
colonel / kernel
council / counsel
creak / creek
crews / cruise
cue / queue
curb / kerb
currant / current
cygnet / signet
days / daze
dear / deer
dew / due
die / dye
died / dyed
dies / dyes
doe / dough
draft / draught
draw / drawer
dying / dyeing
earn / urn
ewe / you / yew
ewes / use
eye / I
eyelet / islet

faint / feint
fair / fare
farther / father
fate / fete
feat / feet
find / fined
fir / fur
flaw / floor
flea / flee
flew / flu / flue
flocks / phlox
flow / floe
flower / flour
for / fore / four
fort / fought
foul / fowl
frays / phrase
freeze / frieze
gait / gate
gamble / gambol
genes / jeans
gild / guild
gnaw / nor
gored / gourd
gorilla / guerrilla
grate / great
grater / greater
groan / grown
guest / guessed
hail / hale
hanger / hangar
hart / heart
heal / heel / he'll
hear / here
heard / herd
hears / here's
hew / hue
higher / hire
him / hymn
ho / hoe
hoard / horde
hoarse / horse
hose / hoes

hole / whole
holy / wholly
hour / our
idle / idol
in / inn
island / Ireland
jam / jamb
key / quay
knave / nave
knead / need / kneed
knew / new
knight / night
knot / not
know / no
knows / nose
lacks / lax
lain / lane
laps / lapse
larva / lava
lead / led
leak / leek
lessen / lesson
liar / lyre
licence / license
lieu / loo / Lou
lightening / lightning
links / lynx
load / lode
loan / lone
loot / lute
made / maid
mail / male
main / mane
maize / maze
mall / maul
manner / manor
mantel / mantle
mare / mayor
marshal / martial
meat / meet / mete
medal / meddle
metal / mettle
metre / meter

Evaluation Sheet

Name: ____________________

Date: ____________________

Criterion	Superior	Satisfactory	Meets requirements	Unsatisfactory
Each assignment conveys a clear and specific purpose				
The student selects facts and composes genres that fit with his or her overall purpose and framing context				
The student successfully identifies and employs the conventions of each chosen genre				
The student places and organises his or her arguments logically				
The student shows connections between different points to support and develop his or her ideas				
The student demonstrates his or her ability to research, select and integrate sources				
The student offers sufficient evidence and explanation to develop his or her main ideas in each genre				

This sheet evaluates the student's writing skills.

Notes: